THE
EXETER CANAL

BY THE SAME AUTHOR

The Kennet & Avon Canal (1968)
The Somersetshire Coal Canal and Railways (1970)
The Dorset & Somerset Canal (1971)
Wessex Waterway (1978)

The Exeter Canal

Kenneth R. Clew

Phillimore

1984

Published by
PHILLIMORE & CO. LTD.
Shopwyke Hall, Chichester, Sussex

ISBN 0 85033 544 2

Printed and bound in Great Britain by
BILLING & SONS LTD
Worcester, England

For Charles Hadfield,
who suggested that I should write the book

CONTENTS

LIST OF PLATES
(between pages 82 and 83)

LIST OF TEXT ILLUSTRATIONS

PREFACE

THE EXETER CANAL is unique. It is the only one in Britain to have remained under the control of local government for more than 400 years. This has been both its strength and its weakness. One of the few canals to escape nationalisation on 1 January 1948, it has been unhindered by decisions of central government. Indeed, the waterway is very much as James Green left it after his alterations and improvements between 1820 and 1830. On the other hand, the crippling burden of the costs of these improvements has conditioned caution in making any further changes.

Whether commercial shipping would still be using the canal if the locks had been lengthened and the sharp curves straightened in the 19th century is a matter of conjecture. If there had been an upsurge in trade, would this have affected the route of the M5 motorway and the height of the viaduct across the waterway? These questions must remain unanswered as, until recently, was the future of the canal. The International Sailing Craft Association (I.S.C.A.) has worked wonders in preserving many of its historic structures since the Exeter Maritime Museum was established in 1969. The formation of the Exeter Canal and Quay Trust by the City Council in 1980 offers new hope for the years to come.

The period covered by this book includes the change from the old style (Julian) calendar to the new style (Gregorian) one in 1752. Until this date the civil and legal New Year began on 25 March. For the convenience of readers, new style dates are used throughout: for example, 4 March 1634-35 is shown as 4 March 1635. I have not attempted to convert pounds, shillings and pence to their decimal equivalents as inflation makes the figures meaningless.

KENNETH R. CLEW

Gillumsfield, April 1984

ACKNOWLEDGEMENTS

EXETER IS FORTUNATE in the vast accumulation of canal records preserved. My grateful thanks go to the archivists and staff of Devon and Somerset Record Offices, and of the former Exeter City Record Office, the librarians and staff of Bath, Exeter and Plymouth Central Libraries, and to the many other people who have helped me in countless different ways. I am particularly grateful to Mrs. M. M. Rowe, County Archivist at Devon Record Office, for reading through the draft of this book; to Charles Hadfield for the use of his files on the Exeter Canal and also reading through the draft; and to David Goddard, Director of Exeter Maritime Museum, for helpful comments on the last chapter. My thanks also go to Alan Voce for transport to and company in walking the banks of the canal and to Glyn Grylls who drew the maps and gave photographic advice. Many others have helped in countless different ways and though I do not list their names I thank them for their generous assistance.

For permission to use their photographs and other illustrations, my thanks go to Devon Library Services: Plates 1, 2, 3, 6, 9 and 12 and Figs. 10 and 14; Devon Record Office: Figs. 2, 4, 6, 7, 11, 12 and 13: International Sailing Craft Association: Plates 4 and 13 and Fig. 16; Mr. A. Mazonowicz: Plate 7; The late Mr. R. W. Nott: Plate 11 and Figs. 8 and 9; Mr. R. W. Shopland and *Waterways World*: Plate 14; Mr. A. P. Voce: Plate 10; *The Western Times*: Plate 5. The remainder are from the author's collection.

My family have cheerfully withstood the isolation when I have been researching and writing this book. Without their tolerance and active co-operation *The Exeter Canal* could not have been written. The imperfections are mine alone.

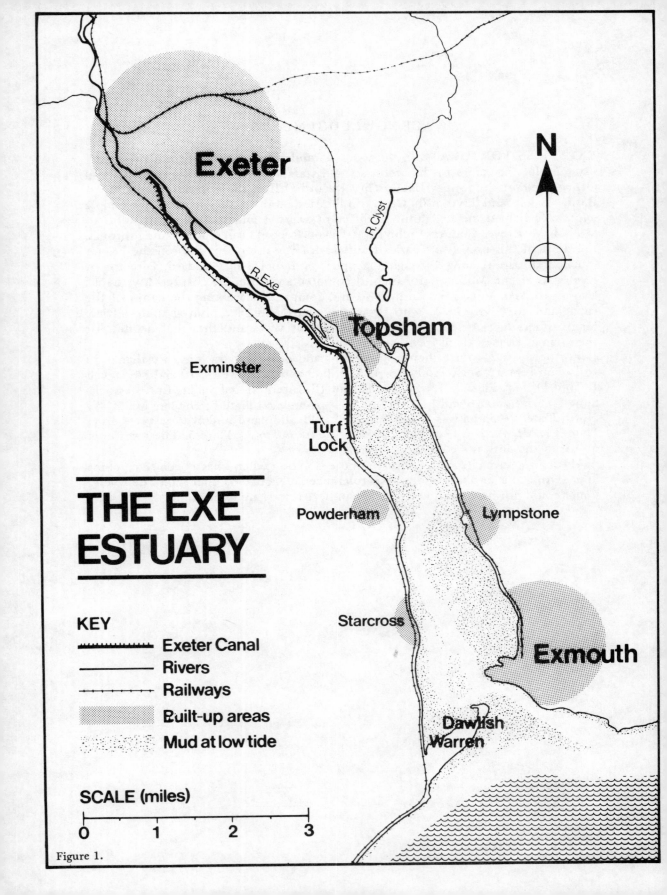

THE EXE ESTUARY

N

Exeter

R.Clyst

R.Exe

Topsham

Exminster

Turf
Lock

Powderham

Lympstone

Starcross

Exmouth

Dawlish
Warren

KEY

ᴡᴡᴡᴡᴡᴡ Exeter Canal
——— Rivers
—ɪ—ɪ— Railways
▒▒▒ Built-up areas
∴∴∴ Mud at low tide

SCALE (miles)

0   1   2   3

Figure 1.

Chapter One

THE LIGHTER CANAL (1539–1697)

SOON AFTER leaving Exeter on the Plymouth-bound train, passengers seated on the left-hand side may see a strange sight—a ship sailing through the middle of the fields. This is no optical illusion but the Exeter Canal, a waterway with a long history stretching back to Tudor times. But to begin at the beginning . . .

The River Exe rises on Exmoor and meanders on its way to reach the sea at Exmouth. The early history of the river is lost in the mists of time, though it is likely that small ships were able to reach the Roman city of Isca Dumnoniorum (as Exeter was then known) on the tide. Isca had been founded about A.D. 50–55 to serve as the administrative centre for the Celtic people of Devon and Cornwall, a tribe known as the Dumnonii. By the 12th century the importance of Exeter had greatly increased. The seat of the bishopric of Devon and Cornwall was transferred from Crediton to Exeter in 1050 and a new cathedral built and consecrated in 1133. The city was one of the first in England to have self-government as a mayor was appointed soon after 1200, the city charters dating from the reign of King Henry II (1154–89).

Although the Exe was only navigable for large ships inland as far as Topsham, smaller craft and barges were able to reach the watergate of the city on the tide. This seaborne trade was soon to be placed in jeopardy by the action of the Courtenay family, Earls of Devon, who began a long struggle for supremacy over the townsfolk of Exeter. It started when Isabella de Fortibus, Countess of Devon, caused a barrier to be built across the river about two miles south of the city (at the place now known as Countess Wear) and so stopped the maritime trade. The reason for this action is not clear. It was perhaps in retaliation for some supposed affront or, more likely, to ensure a monopoly of river tolls because the countess owned the port of Topsham.

Evidently requests for the removal of the barrier were unsuccessful for, at an inquisition held in Exeter during 1290, the jurors of the city stated:

> . . . the water of the Exe belongs to the said city, and of old used to belong, as far as the port of Exmewt; and the great fishery was common to all who wished there, Isabella Countess of Devon, six years ago, raised a certain weir across the water of the Exe at Topsham, and so built it, that the catching of salmon and other fish which used to be caught in the said water this side of the weir was completely stopped, to the grave damage of the city and others in the neighbourhood;

1

and also whereas all kinds of boats used to come up towards the city as far as the bridge of the city with wine and other merchandise, to the great benefit of all the countryside, now no boat can ascend on account of the impediment of the weir to the greatest damage of the said city and of all the neighbourhood.[1]

A later inquisition of 1378 gave a different account of the affair, as the jurors stated that Isabella de Fortibus had first raised a weir or 'heddge' of stakes and thorns near Topsham during the reign of King Henry III (1216–72). A similar weir was constructed on the west side of the river, leaving an opening 30ft. wide in the deepest part of the Exe for ships to pass through on their way to Exeter. Then, in the time of King Edward II (1307–27), Hugh Courtenay, Earl of Devon, increased the height of the weirs by another 12 feet and 'stopped up the said opening of 30 feet with great large and strong timber, stones and other materials'. These obstructions were maintained by his heir, Edward Courtenay, who was Earl of Devon at the time of the inquisition and who constructed two more weirs at Lampreyford and St James'.[2]

It seems likely that the river was first obstructed about the time of King Edward I (1272–1307), to be re-opened following the inquisition of 1290 and that probably the 30-ft. opening was made at that time. A new quay was built at Topsham by Hugh Courtenay in 1316, which gives reason to believe that the river was once more blocked by him after this date, but before 1327.[3]

John Hooker, City Chamberlain, wrote the first book on Exeter about 1590, giving a vivid account of the animosity between Hugh Courtenay and the townsfolk by relating an incident that occurred in 1309. The Earl of Devon had sent one of his servants to buy fish from the market. There were only three baskets available and, because the servants of the Bishop of Exeter also wanted some, the mayor, Roger Beynym, decided upon a compromise. He saved one basket for the earl, another for the bishop and let the third basket go on sale to the townsfolk. The earl was furious, having wanted all the fish for his own use and, considering himself to be grievously affronted, swore that he would exact his revenge.[4]

The opportunity came soon afterwards when Hugh Courtenay stayed at his lodgings within the house of the Black Friars in the city. He sent for the mayor, a retainer of his, to come and speak with him. Roger Beynym, fearing the worst, called a meeting of his friends and the commoners at the Guildhall to explain his predicament. The meeting agreed to accompany him to the earl's lodgings and, if he was detained for more than a short length of time, to force their way into the house to rescue him.

Immediately the mayor entered the earl's lodgings the door was barred and bolted and he was confronted by the furious Hugh Courtenay who refused to listen to reason. Roger Beynym then took off his coat, which bore the livery of the earl, saying that he would wear it no longer. The earl became even more enraged by this action and the mayor began to fear for his safety. Then a knocking began on the outer door. As this was not answered the commoners brought ladders, threatening to break down the doors and rip the house apart unless the mayor was released. The earl gave way to these threats though 'he could never after brooke the Citie nor any Citesan'.

With the blockages of the River Exe at Countess Wear, Lampreyford and St James' all goods bound for Exeter had to be unloaded at Topsham, where they were subject to tolls exacted by the Earl of Devon. The townsfolk of Exeter made many appeals for the removal of these weirs and were successful in legal proceedings, yet nothing was done by the Courtenays because '. . . such was their powre and authoritie and such was the iniquitie of those daies as no justice could take place, nor lawe have his dewe course'.[5]

Of French descent, the Courtenays came to England in 1151 with Eleanor of Aquitaine, the bride of King Henry II, and inherited the Earldom of Devon from cousins in 1293. For the next 250 years they were amongst the most powerful families in the kingdom, providing an Archbishop of Canterbury and a founder Knight of the Garter from their ranks. Occasionally the fortunes of the Courtenays took a turn for the worse, as in 1461 when Thomas Courtenay fell foul of the Crown and was beheaded. The mayor, bailiffs and commonalty of Exeter seized upon this opportunity to petition King Edward IV, complaining of the weirs which prevented shipping from reaching the city and asking that his Council be directed to look into the matter.[6]

The petition went unanswered. Once more the power of the Courtenays seemed to have triumphed as their family fortunes were restored. The townsfolk had to wait for the attainder of Henry Courtenay, Marquess of Exeter, by King Henry VIII in 1538 before their efforts were successful. On 17 October of that year the city chamber (the governing body of the city) ordered 'that suete shalbe made to the kinge and a Byll to be put in to the plament for the newe makinge of the Haven'. In 1539 Henry Courtenay was executed for treason, the same year that Royal Assent was given to 'An Act concerning the amending of the River and Port of Exeter'. At long last the power of the Courtenays had been broken and work could begin to make the river navigable to Exeter once again.[7]

The 1539 Act made no mention of a canal but stated that it would be lawful to:

> . . . plucke downe, digge, moyne, breke, banke, and caste upp all and all manner of weyres, rockes, sandes, gravell, and other lettes and noy-saunces whatsoever they be in the saide river . . . and make all other thinges requisite and necessarie wherby the saide shippes, boates and vessels may have their sure course and recourse in the saide River to & from youre saide Cittie.

These works were considered necessary because of the growth of the woollen trade. This had risen to become the chief industry of Exeter and its neighbourhood, with a thriving export trade in kersey—a coarse-ribbed woollen cloth much favoured by the French. Owing to the blockages of the Exe the cloth had to be taken by road to Topsham, then serving as the port for Exeter. There was little competition, as it was the safest anchorage for many miles. There were no safe harbours on the exposed East Devon coast and, to the west, Teignmouth had its.

entrance almost blocked by a sandbar. Further west there was the natural harbour of Dartmouth, but this was hampered by poor transport facilities inland.

When application was made for the Act to improve the Exe in 1538 the mayor was Henry Hamlyn, an enthusiastic seeker of new markets for the woollen trade. Despite the initial enthusiasm that followed the end of the dominance of the Courtenays, the difficulties arising from more than two centuries of neglect were immense. In 1543 the city chamber appointed four men 'to take charge of the settynge fourth of the worke for the said Haven'. John Hooker, the City Chamberlain, noted that work began in 1546 though this must have been interrupted by the siege of Exeter in 1549. The Act of Uniformity had stipulated that the new *Book of Common Prayer* should be used in all churches from Whit Sunday 1549. A large number of insurgents from Devon and Cornwall, opposed to the introduction of Cranmer's prayer book, marched upon and besieged the city for four weeks. Bridges were destroyed, roads entrenched, some water supplies cut and food supplies began to run short. After a bloody battle at Clyst Heath, near Topsham, the rebels were defeated and Exeter relieved.[8]

In 1551 the city chamber began negotiations with a Mr. Hullond, owner of some mills near Countess Wear which would be deprived of their water supply if the weir was removed. That same year several Exeter parishes gave part of their church plate towards the works, the sale realising £229. These efforts were all in vain, as activity on the project seems to have ceased in 1553.[9]

Seven years later, in 1560, the city chamber reached agreement with William Stroode to improve the river so that 'a Boat laden sufficiently with iiii tonne' could be discharged 'at some Convenient place neere the Citie', the contract to be completed within seven years. Subsequently Stroode agreed that the improvements should be sufficient for a boat laden with eight tons to pass. Again, nothing was done to implement these works.[10]

A third and more successful attempt was made in 1563, with John Trew of Glamorganshire employed to:

> . . . conduct and make the Haven of the Citie in suche sorte as boates
> and vessels laden with Tenne Tonnes vightes at the least shall at all
> tyde & tydes passe & repasse to & from the seas unto the Cities walls.

In return for undertaking these works the city chamber would pay Trew £225 and thereafter give him a percentage of the tolls they received.[11]

Trew's original plan was to follow the existing course of the Exe, using the mill leat to by-pass St James' weir. By the end of the year he had changed his mind and 'thought it better to take the ground away by the weste Syde of the Exe'. The city chamber decided that Edward Bridgeman and others should accompany him on a survey of his revised route. This followed the course of the present canal from about a quarter of a mile south of the city walls to Matford Brook, below Countess Wear, and then improving the river downstream as far as Topsham. The water supply for the canal was to be provided by the construction of a new weir, named Trew's weir after the engineer, which would be built across the Exe just below its junction with the canal at Exeter.[12]

Work began in February 1564, the canal being cut to a width of 16 feet and a depth of 3 feet. There were three pairs of lock gates along its length, so arranged that each pair formed a 'pool' to enable gangs of lighters to pass each other without inconvenience. These pools were over 100ft. long and of much greater width than the remainder of the canal, the lower pool alone being 23ft. wide. They were also deeper, the 5ft. depth allowing the lighters to pass from one level to another through what is thought to have been the first known form of pound lock in Britain. It is doubtful if John Trew recognised the significance, because he had three pairs of lock gates to overcome a rise of only 6 feet in the 3,110 yards length. There was also a single pair of lock gates to the seaward end to retain water in the canal at low tide.[13]

It is probable that the lock gates were at first vertically rising ones, a crude form of the guillotine gates still to be found on the Rivers Cam, Nene, Great Ouse and Yorkshire Derwent, as the lighters had to lower their masts to pass through. However, a report entitled *A Scheme of the Sluces or turnepikes at Exeter Water-workes, a mile of the cittie or thereaboutes, from whence the water runneth toward the sea,* produced about '1630 for the Oxford–Burcot Commission of the River Thames, includes a sketch of the north side of 'ye Sluces'. This shows clearly that these 'sluces' had mitre gates, similar to those used in the conventional form of pound lock.[14]

Included in the improvements was a new quay, complete with a crane, built below the city walls. In January 1566 the city chamber resolved that the duties payable on goods discharged at the quay should be the same as those usually paid at Topsham. Thomas Rawlyns, a tailor, was appointed 'porter & keper of the sayd Water-gate'. The crane was not erected until some time after January 1567 though the canal was probably opened in autumn 1566. It had cost about £5,000 to construct.[15]

With the completion of the lighter canal it was possible for small boats to reach Exeter once more. Goods were unloaded from sea-going ships anchored in the Exe estuary off Topsham and then taken up the canal in a fleet of lighters owned by the city chamber. Local boats of limited tonnage were also permitted to use the lighter canal. It was soon found that the new water-way was not the success that had been expected, because boats were only able to enter it at high tides without any difficulty. The river from the head of the canal to the new quay also tended to silt. Urgent action was required, and in July 1567 repairs of the 'Haven' costing £100 were approved, these being financed by money borrowed from William Martyn at 10 per cent. interest.[16]

The repairs took longer than expected and were not completed within the agreed time of one year, so the term of the loan was extended to August 1568. John Trew was in disgrace and the inevitable litigation took place when he attempted to obtain his fees. This dispute dragged on until 1573, the city chamber then agreeing that 'M. Geffrey Tothill & others shall have the Commission & authoritie to deale for Trewe'. By this time Trew was almost penniless and he wrote to Lord Burleigh about his case:

. . . The varyableness of men, and the great injury done unto me, brought
me in such case that I wyshed my credetours sattisfyed and I away
from earth: what becom may of my poor wyf & children, who lye in
great mysery, for that I have spent all.

There was a happy end to this story as Trew later accepted a cash sum of £224
and a yearly rent or annuity of £30 in settlement of his claim.[17]

The city chamber were soon to be involved in another law suit, this time with
the lessees of Topsham quay, as the Courtenays' interest in it had passed to the
Crown in 1535. They had suffered a loss of trade when the canal opened, because
ships laden with goods for Exeter now anchored in mid-river to discharge their
cargoes into lighters and no longer used the quay. The lessees claimed dues on
all craft, whether or not they used the quay, and used force to assert their rights,
severely injuring one of the lightermen in the process. Eventually, in 1580, a
compromise was reached and it was agreed that dues should only be paid to
Topsham for goods unloaded at that quay, though the city chamber would make
a yearly payment of 20 marks as compensation for the loss of trade to the canal.
In 1583 the city chamber gained control of Topsham quay by buying up the
remaining period of the lease, but failed to retain it when it came up for renewal
in 1614.

In the meantime the city chamber was having more trouble with the canal,
particularly by silting. In June 1579 they resolved:

. . . that M. Hutchins & ors on Mondaye or Tuesday next with M. Hoker
shall view the watercourse or newe Haven & consider how farre the
same is to be cutt for the better making of the said Haven.

A major reconstruction took place in 1581, these alterations costing £368.[18]

Most of the import trade consisted of bulky goods such as coal, timber and
wine. When quick delivery was required it was usual to unload the goods at
Topsham quay and then send them overland to Exeter. This route was used in
the reverse direction for the export of serge cloth when ships were available and
waiting at Topsham quay. One reason why road transport was often preferred
to the canal was that the latter was frequently leased during the early years of its
history and the lessees did not always maintain it to a reasonable standard. There
were more complaints about silting in March 1619, of stones lying in the river
near Topsham in August 1630, and of 'some Decaye in the bank of the Haven'
in November of the following year.[19]

In March 1634 there was trouble with the locks and further repairs were
sanctioned:

Whereas there is a Beame lately broken in one of the Sluices which is
very Prejudiciall to the passage of the Boates through the Haven, it is
this day agreed that Mr. Receiver shall cause a tree fit for the amend-
ment thereof to be felled in Duryard Wood forthwith and shall cause
the said Sluice to be sufficiently repaired and also all other defects in
the said Haven or new Worke as shall be needful on his judgement.[20]

When repairs were made the canal often had to be closed for long periods, as in 1635 when the replacement of a sluice took 25 days. During these closure periods there was no alternative but to turn to road transport. The neglect of the canal by the lessees accentuated this move, one having been said to have neglected 'clensinge and scouringe' for no less than 13 years.

Trade took a disastrous turn for the worse with the outbreak of the Civil War (1642-46). The canal banks suffered from the effects of galloping horses, the mounted troops of cavalry breaking them down in several places. Lack of attention to the lock gates for long periods brought further problems of flooding. It is not surprising that the receipts from canal dues fell to £56 in 1644 and £33 in 1645, compared with the £230 per annum received from the canal lease before the start of the Civil War.

Extensive repairs were made in 1646, though they failed to restore the canal to its former condition. More troubles were caused by the combination of an inefficient lessee who neglected maintenance and an enterprising mill owner. The mill owner, George Browning, built a fulling mill for serge cloth on the river bank just below Trew's Weir. To provide power for his mill he cut a 58-ft. wide leat from the river above the weir, which rejoined the river below the weir. It was completed in 1663 and the consequences for canal traffic were predictable. The leat damaged part of the weir and river bank, the canal being closed for a month through shortage of water. Subsequent attempts to work the mill caused barges to be grounded and traffic delayed for weeks at a time. For seven years the city chamber were engaged in a series of law suits to close it down and success came at last in 1670. Constant vigilance was still required, because Browning attempted to work the mill in defiance of the court order for almost another 20 years.

There was a separate threat to the supremacy of Exeter as a port, arising from the long-standing rivalry with Topsham. In 1663 the custom officials asked that the Custom House be moved to Topsham, where it would be more convenient for all craft using the Exe estuary. Their petition was granted by the Lord Treasurer, who authorised the erection of a new Custom House at Topsham. Exeter immediately appealed to the Privy Council at this decision and was successful in retaining its own Custom House. One of the advocates of the city's cause was the Secretary of State, Sir William Morice, whose son was afterwards appointed the collector of customs at Exeter.

The canal needed urgent improvements if it was to compete with the alternative of road transport. The city chamber were well aware of the problem, and in 1671 called a conference to consider 'the enlarging of the new haven'. A Dutch engineer was consulted, and later still, Richard Hurd, an engineer from Cardiff, was engaged. Work began in 1676, when the existing canal lease expired. The improvements consisted of thoroughly dredging the canal and extending it a further half a mile towards Topsham by cutting a channel through the Exminster marshes. This saved a mile of difficult river nagivation, for previously the canal had ended just below Countess Wear and now terminated just above Topsham.

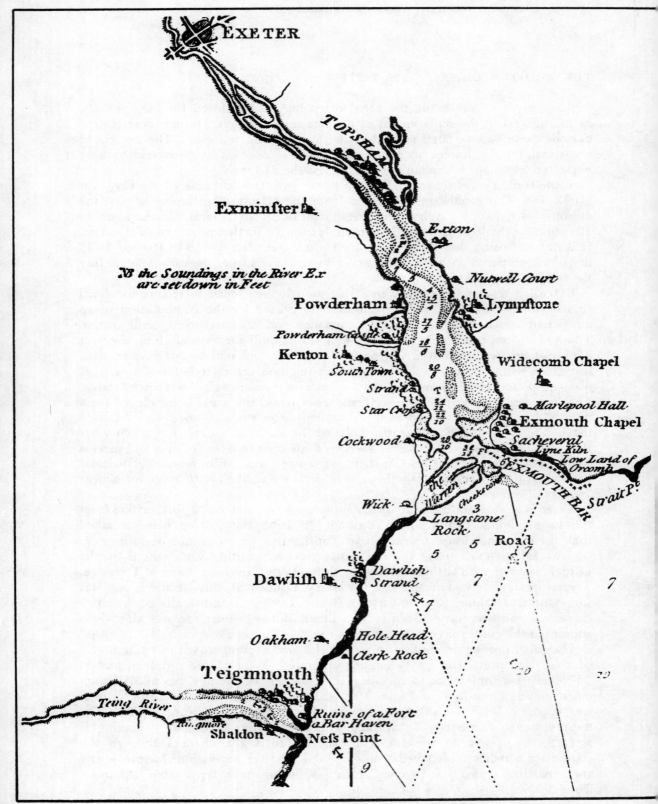

Figure 2. Chart of the Exe and Teign estuaries in 1679.

The new entrance was equipped with a single pair of lock gates and was at first known as Topsham sluice. Later the name was changed to Trenchard's sluice, after its lock-keeper. These gates gave entrance to a large transhipment basin, capable of holding at least 50 sea-going vessels. Here their cargoes could more easily be unloaded into lighters than if they were to be anchored in the Exe estuary. A new and stronger weir was built near Trew's weir and the quay at Exeter greatly enlarged. The improvements were all completed within a year and it is recorded that the first lighter to use the reconstructed canal came with 'her full loadinge to the Key of Exeter to the Admiration of the Spectators'. The cost of the extension, including the purchase of the land required and the other improvements, was between £3,000 and £5,000. Richard Hurd received a fee of £100 for his services.[21]

Rates for the carriage of liquid goods (e.g. wine) were reduced from 5s. 0d. to 2s. 6d. per ton, and to 2s. 0d. per ton for all other goods brought to the quay except coal, the latter being charged 1s. 0d. per quarter. These new rates brought alarm to the lessees of Topsham quay, who began an action against the city chamber in 1678. They alleged that the river in front of their own quay had been blocked by stones and mud excavated by Richard Hurd. This was countered by the accusation that the Topsham men had caused the blockage themselves, by throwing their own rubbish into the river. The result of the litigation is not known, though Exeter's supremacy as a port was enhanced by the building of a new Custom House at the quay in 1681.[22]

Prior to 1675 the canal had been leased for £130 per annum, a figure increased to £800 per annum by 1691. A daily lighter service was now possible, compared with former times when it took up to a week to pass through the canal. Most of the increased trade was due to the rapid rise in exports of serge cloth. This rose from 153,435lbs. in 1666 to 1,307,239lbs. in 1676, and 1,718,977lbs. in 1686.[23]

Even with the improvements, the canal still remained limited to lighters not exceeding 16 tons. The defects of its design once more became apparent as silting reoccurred, limiting navigation at neap tides to lighters of under 10 tons burthen. The city chamber took action in 1696, deputing two of their members 'to treat with some Engineers now here in the City about ye enlarging of the Haven & the bringing upp ships to the Key'. In January 1697 they decided to make the canal navigable for ships of 100 tons, but nothing could be done until the existing lease expired in August 1698.[24]

Celia Fiennes, who visited Exeter on her journeys in 1698, gave the reasons for this decision when she wrote about the lighter canal:

> . . . they are attempting to make navigable to the town which will be of mighty advantage to have shipps come up close to the town to take in their serges, which now they are forced to send to Topsham on horses by land.[25]

The stage was set for a new lease of life as a ship canal.

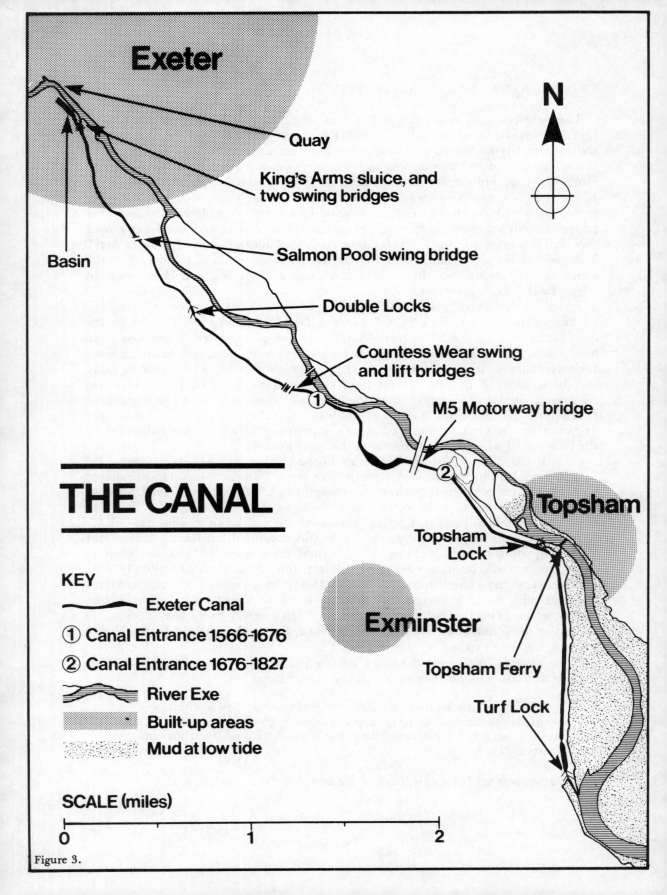

THE CANAL

Exeter

Quay

King's Arms sluice, and
two swing bridges

Salmon Pool swing bridge

Double Locks

Basin

Countess Wear swing
and lift bridges

①

M5 Motorway bridge

②

Topsham

Topsham
Lock

Exminster

Topsham Ferry

Turf Lock

N

KEY

⎯⎯⎯ Exeter Canal

① Canal Entrance 1566-1676

② Canal Entrance 1676-1827

River Exe

Built-up areas

Mud at low tide

SCALE (miles)

0   1   2

Figure 3.

Chapter Two

THE SHIP CANAL (1698–1819)

IN SEPTEMBER 1698 the city chamber made an agreement with William Bayley, an engineer from Winchester. He was to widen the canal to 42 feet at water-level and deepen it to 14 feet, so that it could be used by sea-going ships of 60 tons burthen. The lock gates, apart from the one at Trenchard's sluice, were to be removed, and the three small locks replaced by one double-width lock known as 'Double locks'. It was to be 350ft. long and up to 75ft. wide. Trew's weir was to be enlarged, the canal banks widened to make towing easier, and alterations made to prevent flood water from the Alphington Brook reaching the canal. The channel of the River Exe from Trenchard's sluice to Topsham was also to be deepened and, if thought necessary by the city chamber within three years of the completion of these works, Bayley was to extend the canal to Turf reach.[1]

By 1699 the city chamber was concerned about progress and made arrangements 'to View & judge how far Mr. Bayley the Engineer hath proceeded in making the new works'. They had a surprise because Bayley had fled, taking with him some of the city's money and leaving the canal in a ruinous and impassable condition. Efforts were made to repossess as much of the canal property as was possible, the city chamber ordering:

> . . . Mr. Aldn. Coke & Mr. Hooper the Carpenter do forthwithe go to Pagewell in Devon & there Seize on & secure such Timber as was there lately bought by Mr. Bayley the Engineer & paid for by the Chamber & cause the same to be brought hither and used in the new Work.

Similarly, Peter Trenchard the lock-keeper was told to 'take care to get back such Timber as hath lately been carried away from the Sluices'. Compassion was shown to the workmen employed by William Bayley, for their wages had been embezzled, and it was decided that 'for their day labor be paid every one of them 2s. 6d. as a free gift from the Chamber'. They were also to be employed in digging the canal two feet deeper.[2]

It was particularly unfortunate that the canal closure should have occurred when the serge cloth trade was booming, a fact underlined by Celia Fiennes who wrote that it produced 'the most money in a weeke of anything in England'. Road transport rates doubled, for though the War of the League of Augsburg against France (1688–97) had caused the loss of the French woollen trade, there were new markets in the Netherlands, Germany, Spain and Portugal to compensate. Exeter's prosperity was based on export markets for its serge cloth, and the war with France was a reminder that this trade depended on a peaceful co-existence with other European countries and, of course, the ability to compete with other producers. Both lessons were to be ignored in the next century.[3]

In June 1699 Daniel Durell was appointed engineer, being paid £3 per week to complete the canal. Voluntary help was given by the people of Exeter:

> . . . The parishes of St Stephen and St Lawrence wrought each one day; the several Corporations did work by turns, having a drum beaten before them in the evening, when they went home from work. The men of Alphington and St David's did also each of them work one day a-piece; and after them they of St Sidwell's parish wrought one day; the men and women of Trinity parish one day; married women and young women, decked with ribbons; the parishes of St Petrock's and St Keryan's one day; the parish of St Mary the More one day, men and women; the worsted combers one day; the parishes did provide their dinner for them.[4]

Despite the voluntary labour, finance was still needed, and in November 1699 the city chamber had to stop work until further notice. In January 1700 an attempt was made to obtain an Act of Parliament to raise money 'for perfecting the making the River Exe navigable'. Some £10,000 had been spent on the canal in the preceding 25 years and a further £11,000 during the past two years. The cost of completing it was estimated to be another £5,000, but owing to opposition from some of the inhabitants of Exeter the mayor and city chamber did not persist with their application for an Act.[5]

The city chamber then decided to borrow the money, the loans including a mortgage of £500 upon the 'Town Customs'. In July 1700 they had raised sufficient cash and ordered that 'the Water Works already begun in order to bring up Ships to this City to be carried on with Vigour'. The canal was re-opened in 1701, new tolls having been agreed in January of that year. These included passage dues of 5s. 0d. for ships and 2s. 6d. for lighters using the canal to Exeter quay. Additional dues of 2s. 6d. per ton for ships and 2s. 0d. per ton for lighters were made for all goods carried aboard the craft.[6]

The completed canal included a number of changes from the plans originally agreed with William Bayley. It was now only 10ft. deep but 50ft. wide, sufficient for coasters and small sea-going ships of up to 150 tons burthen. A new pair of flood-gates, known as King's Arm sluice, was provided at the Exeter end of the canal at the junction between the canal and the river. The three old pairs of lock gates were removed and replaced by 'Double locks' which also served as a passing place. This was about two miles from the entrance to the canal, now renamed Lower sluice in place of its former name of Trenchard's sluice.

One of the difficulties encountered when larger craft began to use the canal was the evasion of tolls. Shipmasters with large cargoes would load or unload part of them at Exeter without the knowledge of the wharfinger and then give a false declaration of the amount. The chief offenders appeared to be the canny

Devon captains engaged in the carriage of slate from Dartmoor. To avoid these losses the city chamber imposed an additional toll of 10s. 0d. on any boat which unloaded slate or shingle stone at Exeter quay without prior notice to the wharfinger. Five years later, in 1709, the additonal toll was doubled, showing that the enterprise of a county which bred the Elizabethan sea-dogs was far from dead. Even so, difficulties in collecting tolls continued for many years, and in 1726 it was decided that 'all persons that refuse to pay the Town Duty to be forthwith sued'.[7]

Between 1715 and 1724 an average of 300 craft a year passed up the canal, over half of them being lighters laden with coal. Other imports included cider, timber, slates, groceries from London and Bristol, and goods from southern Europe. Serge cloth continued to be the principal export, for which the main markets were Germany, the Low Countries, Spain, Portugal and Italy.[8]

Although the ship canal was a great improvement on the former lighter canal, many of the old problems remained—particularly that of silting. The approach to Lower sluice was along an artificial channel, cut from the main estuary near Topsham. This was tidal and the largest ships were only able to enter the canal at spring tides. There were also problems with silting at Exeter quay, and the committee for quay affairs were asked by the city chamber 'to view the Works and deepen the same' in 1729.[9]

The canal was closed on several occasions during the first half of the 18th century whilst major repairs were undertaken. In 1707 Lower sluice was rebuilt, in 1727 there was a three months' closure whilst King's Arms sluice was replaced, and in 1753 new lock gates were fitted at Double locks. To pay for these major repairs it was often necessary to borrow money; £1,000 was lent at 4 per cent. interest in 1753. In 1754 the Custom House quay and other premises at Exeter were mortgaged for £8,000 at 3½ per cent. interest to meet the cost of further repairs.

The year 1750 saw 479 craft pass up the canal to Exeter quay, of which 298 were lighters. Of the others, only three were engaged in overseas trade as almost all of the large ships loaded and unloaded at Topsham. Waggons had linked this port with Exeter for the first time in 1725 and many Exeter merchants used Topsham in preference to the canal. The city chamber were sufficiently concerned to purchase Topsham quay in 1769. The major import through the Exeter Canal was still coal, which accounted for 190 of the cargoes in 1750. Soon afterwards there was a possibility that even this trade might be affected, as coal was discovered at Cleave, near Exeter. A mine was sunk, and in 1754 a prospectus issued inviting people to become shareholders. Those who subscribed a guinea were promised a delivery of four quarters of coal if and when the mine became a commercial proposition. The more affluent who subscribed five guineas were promised 20 quarters of coal and the additional privilege of inspecting the books of the enterprise! There were few willing to speculate on this venture and no more was heard of it.[10]

Another scheme which could have affected the trade of the canal was the Exeter & Uphill Canal project. In 1768 a group of Taunton men asked James

Brindley to survey the route for a canal to link the Bristol Channel with the English Channel. The survey was undertaken by Robert Whitworth, under James Brindley's direction, and was for a barge canal from either Topsham or Exeter via Cullompton or Tiverton to Wellington and Taunton. Here it would connect with the Tone Navigation and use that line as far as Burrow Bridge, a second canal being cut from that point to Uphill, near Weston-super-Mare, by way of Bridgwater, Glastonbury, Wells and Axbridge. Again, nothing became of the project.[11]

Major repairs were needed for Lower sluice during the winter of 1790–91, causing the canal to be closed for over six months. To retain the lighter traffic a dam was thrown across the waterway above Lower sluice and an opening cut through the bank, enabling small craft to enter on the spring tides. During the 38 years from 1758 to 1795 maintenance costs came to more than £33,000. Of this sum, no less than £13,000 was spent in the decade from 1786.[12]

Coal provided about two-thirds of the overall receipts between 1786 and 1795, averaging £2,200 a year. The principal export was still serge cloth, though this industry was soon to go into decline as a result of the Napoleonic Wars. Apart from a brief respite during the Peace of Amiens (1802–3), Britain was at war continuously from 1792 to 1814. With its chief markets closed, the serge cloth industry had to look elsewhere and found a new sales outlet in the East India Company. The volume of exports actually increased during the last years of the 18th century, although the overall market was contracting.[13]

A more immediate threat to the home trade came from the 'Canal Mania' of 1792–93. This was a time when a multiplicity of new canal schemes was promoted and advertised, speculators flocking to invest in shares following the success of earlier waterways. For example, the Birmingham Canal paid a dividend of over 23 per cent. in 1789. Two schemes, the Grand Western Canal and the Public Devonshire Canal, were planned to link Exeter with Topsham, whilst a third, the Exeter & Crediton Navigation, was promoted in the utmost secrecy.

Had the Exeter Canal been more efficiently worked and maintained at this time it is doubtful if the alternative routes between Topsham and Exeter would ever have reached the planning stage. The long closure of over six months during winter 1790–91 to all but lighter traffic meant that sea-going ships had to discharge their cargoes at Topsham quay. Though the quay had been purchased by the city chamber in 1769, the chief beneficiaries of the long closure were the carters who transported the goods onwards to Exeter by road. The time was right for an alternative to the ship canal, and the canal mania provided the impetus.

On 1 October 1792 a meeting 'for the Consideration of making a Navigable Canal from Taunton to Topsham' was held at the *Half Moon Inn*, Cullompton. The proposed route from Topsham, via the Clyst valley to Clyst Hydon, then by way of the Culm valley towards Cullompton, Sampford Peverell, Wellington and Taunton was approved, as were proposals for short branches to the outskirts of Exeter and to Cullompton, with a longer branch to connect Tiverton with the main line near Sampford Peverell. Henry Brutton, attorney at Cullompton, was appointed secretary and solicitor to the undertaking and it was resolved to hold a further meeting at the end of the month, to enable the land proprietors, merchants and manufacturers to attend.[14]

This second meeting was held at the *White Hart Inn*, Cullompton, on 29 October when it was resolved that a survey be undertaken and estimates made of the cost. A committee was formed and subscription books opened for the shares of £100 each, 90 people subscribing a total of £73,200 at the meeting and paying a first call of one guinea on each share. By November the undertaking had become known as the Grand Western Canal, and soon afterwards John Longbothom, a former pupil of John Smeaton, was engaged to survey the route.[15]

Robert Whitworth's plans for the earlier Exeter & Uphill Canal project, which had, seemingly, formed the basis for the Grand Western Canal project, were not forgotten. They were advertised to be published on 31 March 1793 by John Cary, 181 Strand, London, at 2s. 6d. This was an opportune time, for two schemes were afoot to link Taunton with the Bristol Channel. The first of these, the Bristol & Western Canal, was planned to link the Bristol Avon at Morgan's Pill with Taunton. It was promoted at Wells, Somerset, on 5 December 1792 in conditions of great secrecy. This caused much annoyance, especially as the subscription books had been filled by speculators, and in January 1793 a meeting at Taunton revived the Taunton to Uphill section of the Exeter & Uphill Canal project. An attempt by the Bristol & Western Canal committee to join the two projects together was rejected, and John Longbothom and William White, who had been asked by the Bristol & Western to survey their route, chose one very similar to that proposed for the Taunton to Uphill scheme. In 1794 Jessop also looked over the Taunton & Uphill line.

Both the Bristol & Western and Taunton & Uphill committees attempted to gain the support of the Grand Western Canal committee for their respective schemes. Neither was to come to fruition. The Bristol & Western (now Bristol & Taunton) Bill was defeated in Parliament in 1796 and the project abandoned. The Taunton & Uphill had failed earlier, in 1794, owing to the opposition of the landowners.[16]

Longbothom completed his survey of the Grand Western Canal in June 1793, estimating the cost as £166,724, this sum including the branches. As it was more than the share capital already subscribed, a second issue of shares of £100 was offered to the original subscribers and a further £71,200 raised. The committee also decided that 'a revisal of the plans and estimates completed be made', choosing Robert Mylne, engineer of the Gloucester & Berkeley Canal. Later still, when Mylne's report was ready, they asked William Jessop, the foremost expert on canals, for his opinion on the various proposals and estimates.[17]

Jessop was helped in this task by Hugh Henshall, brother-in-law of the late James Brindley, and the report was ready for presentation to the committee on 28 November 1793. Jessop favoured Longbothom's proposals, but recommended the omission of the branches to Cullompton and Tiverton as they were unlikely to make a profit. He criticised the proposal that the canal be built with narrow locks, noting that 'a principal Object of this Canal is ultimately to make a Junction with the Bristol Channel'. If wide locks were built, at an additional cost of £5,000, it would be possible for decked boats of up to 15-ft. beam to carry a maximum of 50 tons of coal from the Welsh ports across the Bristol Channel in complete safety. He sounded a note of warning:

> . . . that much of the Success of this Scheme depends on the Event of an Extension from Taunton to Bristol; and that also has a mutual Dependance on this. It would probably be best for both if they were united as One Concern.

His own personal preference was for the Taunton & Uphill Canal project, describing it 'as the easiest Line for a Canal that I have ever seen'.

Two observations in his report posed a threat to the profitability of the Exeter Canal:

> . . . It seems to be generally understood, that to make this Canal productive to the Undertakers, it is essential that Coal should be obtained and conveyed at such a Price as to supply some Part of the Consumption at Exeter . . . and all the Towns and Villages short of Exeter, including Tiverton, Honiton, and Crediton, will certainly be supplied from the Canal.

Jessop estimated that coal could be brought from Wales to Exeter via the Taunton & Uphill and Grand Western canals for 19s. 4½d. per ton, compared with the £1 4s. 0d. then being charged for coal from Newcastle and Liverpool.[18]

At a general meeting of the Grand Western Canal subscribers on 16 December 1793 it was decided 'that the plan and survey of Mr. Longbothom of the intended canal, as corrected by Mr. Jessop, be approved of, and the same be carried into execution'. Not everyone was content, for the city chamber was worried about competition with their own canal. The Exeter coal trade would be affected and the proposed reservoirs for the Grand Western, to be fed from the River Culm, could interrupt or reduce the water supply to the Exeter Canal, partially fed from the same source. In an attempt to overcome these objections the Grand Western Canal committee asked John Rennie, engineer to the Kennet & Avon Canal, to give his opinion and make an alternative survey.

Rennie suggested a number of changes to the route agreed, including the reinstatement of the branches to Cullompton and Tiverton, but omitting the one to the Exeter road which was the subject of concern by the city chamber. Surveys taken by two engineers, Charles Wedge and Josiah Easton, under Rennie's direction had shown that fears of a water shortage were groundless. The revised estimate for this route, including the branches, was £211,875. This increase can partly be explained by the inflationary effects of the Napoleonic Wars. The subscribers approved the changes at a general meeting on 13 July 1795 and resolved to apply for the necessary Act of Parliament for the canal.[19]

The changes did not satisfy the city chamber, though the abandonment of the branch from Sowton to the Exeter road would mean that all coal would be carried through to Topsham and then sent to Exeter via the Exeter Canal. The city would gain both by an increase in trade and a reduction in the price of coal. However, the additional competition could lose the Exeter Canal up to £1,000 per annum in trade, and so the city chamber petitioned against the Grand Western Canal Bill, claiming:

> . . . the said Canal, between Topsham and Exeter, established at so great an Expence by the Petitioners, for promoting the Trade and Commerce of a Place so important as the City of Exeter, and the several Interests before-mentioned ought not in Justice to be broken in upon, or put in Hazard by any new Speculation.[20]

The Grand Western committee then made a compromise with the city chamber, agreeing to make good any loss of dues upon the Exeter Canal. The Grand Western Canal Act of 1796 gave further protection by forbidding the landing of coal at any point within six miles of Exeter. Financial prospects for the new canal seemed less promising now that the Act had been passed. The dream of a through route to the Bristol Channel had been shattered by the collapse of the Taunton & Uphill project in 1794, followed by the failure of the Bristol & Western Canal Bill in 1796. These factors, coupled with rising inflation, caused the postponement of any work on the Grand Western Canal for over a decade. The canal mania was over.[21]

The two other canal schemes that concerned Exeter, the Exeter & Crediton Navigation and the Public Devonshire Canal, did not cause any noticeable concern to the city chamber. For this reason, and because the fortunes of both were closely connected, their story is told in the following chapter.

A revival of the Grand Western Canal came in July 1808 when a meeting of the shareholders was held, two of their number being appointed to investigate the prospects for the commencement of construction work. A year earlier the Kennet & Avon Canal proprietors had been asked for financial help but, with money troubles of their own, they had to refuse assistance. However, all 903 unappropriated Grand Western Canal shares were purchased by some of the Kennet & Avon proprietors in 1810. The reason for this speculation became clear at a special meeting of the Grand Western Canal shareholders on 12 April 1810 at the *Half Moon Inn,* Cullompton. Besides agreeing that work should start at once, with John Rennie as engineer, they also decided that a new canal should be promoted to provide a link to Bristol at an expense not exceeding £330,000. One-third of the shares of this, at first known as the Bristol & Western Union and later as the Bristol & Taunton, were reserved for the Grand Western Canal proprietors and another third for the Kennet & Avon Canal proprietors.[22]

A contemporary pamphlet noted the advantages of the Bristol & Taunton Canal:

> . . . it is proposed to make the Canal from BRISTOL to TAUNTON of the same dimensions as the *Kennet & Avon* Canal and the *Grand Western* Canal; so that barges of *fifty tons* burthen may be laden at EXETER, and proceed to LONDON (a distance upwards of 200 miles) without shifting their cargoes.[23]

Acts for the Bristol & Taunton and for a new Bath & Bristol Canal received the Royal Assent in 1811. Neither was cut. In the meantime the Grand Western Canal proprietors wasted no time in starting work on their own waterway. The first sod was ceremoniously cut on the summit level in the parish of Holcombe Rogus by the chairman, Sir George Yonge, Bt., on Monday, 16 April 1810. It had been decided that the Lowdwells (near Holcombe Rogus) to Tiverton section should be completed first, a large trade in limestone being anticipated along this part of the route. Cutting proved to be more expensive than expected, the cost being £244,505. This was far more than Rennie's estimate for the entire route from Topsham to Taunton.

The 11 miles of the Grand Western Canal from Lowdwells to Tiverton opened to traffic on 25 August 1814 and, by then, thoughts of completing the route westwards towards Topsham had long been discounted. The route eastwards from Lowdwells to Taunton was not completed until 1838 and in 1867 it was abandoned, following the sale of the entire canal to the Bristol & Exeter Railway in 1864. The remaining portion continues in use for pleasure cruising by unpowered craft, having been transferred in 1971 to Devon County Council.[24]

The Grand Western Canal no longer offered a threat to the trade of the Exeter Canal, but the city chamber still had troubles to resolve. Frequent repairs were necessary, but their canal remained impassable at neap tides to craft bigger than lighters. Sometimes a neap tide gave the opportunity for closure for essential maintenance work and to remove silt from the canal bed. The major problem was the single pair of lock gates at the seaward end of the waterway. In 1801, and again in 1805, the city chamber had considered fitting a second pair of lock gates at Lower sluice, but no firm action was taken to carry this into effect.

The preparations required to take a ship from Exeter quay through the canal were graphically described in a contemporary newspaper. As it was emptied at low tide, so that adjacent meadowlands could be drained:

> . . . it was necessary to give notice to the keeper of the lower sluice to shut his gate at high water; then it was necessary also to give notice to the keeper of the double lock to draw water from the upper reach to fill the whole of the lower reach to the height of five or six feet additionally, according as the tide has risen. This delay sometimes cost a vessel two or three tides, before she could get into the tideway of the Exe; by that time the wind might have shifted, and she might be detained a considerable period, perhaps (as has often been the case) weeks, before a favourable wind returned; when but for these impediments she might have cleared the bar, and proceeded to sea at once.[25]

Changes were soon to come, the first affecting the city chamber. At a meeting on 13 December 1814 they appointed a navigation committee for the canal. This was to meet on the first Monday of each month, the senior member present to take the chair at 12.30 p.m. An allowance of four guineas was made for the expenses of the committee, but those not present at 1 p.m. were to be barred from the meeting and fined 2s. 6d. unless they were away on business at least ten miles from Exeter.[26]

The possibility of adding a second pair of lock gates at Lower sluice was raised again in 1815, in 1818, and in a petition from the traders and merchants of Exeter in 1820. No action was taken, though the navigation committee considered that the advice of 'some eminent Engineers' should be sought on improvements to the canal. In 1819 new lock gates were fitted to Lower sluice at a cost of £370, yet it still remained with just a single pair. This same year saw the appointment of James Green, Surveyor of Bridges and Buildings for the County of Devon, to report and recommend improvements 'for bettering the navigation'.

It was a good choice, for Green had worked under Rennie for many years before his appointment in Devon. In 1810 he had produced plans for the Torrington or Rolle Canal, later to be built under his supervision in 1824–25. He was also engineer of the Exeter & Crediton Navigation and was later to be concerned in making surveys for the Liskeard & Looe Union and Chard canals.

The time for action over the ship canal had at last begun.

CANAL

FROM

ʃopʃham to Exeter, Crediton, &c.

>>>>>>><<<<<<<

NOTICE is hereby given, That a PUBLIC MEETING will be held at the SHIP INN, in CREDITON, on Tueʃday the 5th day of February next, by Eleven o'clock in the forenoon, to conʃider of the propriety of cutting a Canal from *Topʃham* to *Exeter*, *Crediton*, and as much farther as ʃhall appear to be for the advantage of the Public, at which all PERSONS wiʃhing to forward an undertaking ʃo apparently laudable and advantageous, are deʃired to attend.

Dated *January* 24, 1793.

THE PUBLIC muʃt be convinced of the neceʃʃity and propriety of this Meeting, and of its being as general as poʃʃible, by referring to certain Reʃolutions relating to a Canal from *Exeter* to *Crediton*, which have appeared in the public papers, and on which it is only neceʃʃary to remark, that the Gentlemen forming that Society have (perhaps without thoroughly weighing the conʃequences) taken up the affair in a private and very limited manner, omitting to conʃult and intereʃt the Public, who in all *ʃimilar* undertakings have been invariably reʃorted to. No reflection is, however, meant to be caʃt on the very reʃpectable *Landowners*, who have given their countenance to the Society already formed; becauʃe, from their well-known characters, it is preʃumed, that when it ʃhall be clearly proved that the Plan they have been preʃented with, is partial and monopolizing, and that *another*, more extenʃively beneficial, can with great facility be executed, they will be ready to give their effectual ʃupport to *that*, which has the moʃt powerful claim for it.

N. B. SUBSCRIPTIONS will be opened and entered into at the ʃaid Meeting, if it ʃhall then appear expedient.

Executed by S. WOOLMER, Printer of the EXETER GAZETTE.

Figure 4.   Handbill for meeting to promote the Public Devonshire Canal.

Chapter Three

CANALS TO CREDITON (1792–1819)

IN NOVEMBER 1792 the news columns of an Exeter newspaper reported 'It is supposed that a Navigable Canal between Exeter and Crediton, would be of great public utility, and that it might be made at no very great expence'. Nothing more was heard of this until January 1793 when the same newspaper carried an advertisement headed 'CANAL FROM EXETER TO CREDITON'. This gave details of a meeting of 'the Subscribers to this Undertaking' held on 19 January 1793. Significantly, the venue was not stated, though the meeting had resolved that 'a Navigable Canal from Exeter to Crediton, would be of great public Utility and Advantage' and that subscriptions should be immediately opened. Shares of £100 were agreed, with a maximum of ten and minimum of one per subscriber and 'a considerable sum immediately raised'. It was decided that a survey and estimates be made, including the possibility of extending the canal beyond Crediton.[1]

At first glance this scheme appears to have been just one of the many promoted during the time of the canal mania. There was one vital difference—nobody had prior knowledge of the event apart from the subscribers to the undertaking.

Reaction was swift and inevitable, coming with the publication of a handbill on the day that the news of the meeting had appeared (*see* opposite). This advertised a public meeting at the *Ship Inn,* Crediton, on Tuesday, 5 February 'to consider of the propriety of cutting a Canal from Topsham to Exeter, Crediton, and as much farther as shall appear to be for the advantage of the Public'. Referring to the earlier meeting of subscribers to the canal from Exeter to Crediton, it commented that:

> . . . the Gentlemen forming that Society have (perhaps without thoroughly weighing up the consequences) taken up the affair in a private and very limited manner, omitting to consult and interest the Public, who in all *similar* undertakings have been invariably resorted to.[2]

One person who played a leading part in the plans for this rival canal was Christopher Hamlyn of Colebrooke. Prior to the public meeting at Crediton he wrote to John Houghton, clerk to the Birmingham Canal, seeking his advice about the problems of canal cutting. Houghton's reply was full of sound commonsense, warning about deviations from the agreed plan for the 'gratification of selfish individuals'. He noted that work done by contract had been found to be the worst mode that could be adopted and sounded a word of warning about the engineering profession: 'it abounds with quacks and pretenders and but few of Sterling Merit'. These strictures did not apply to Robert Whitworth who had, apparently, been engaged to advise on the route of the intended canal, Houghton commenting 'he is a person of long Experience and very Capable'.[3]

Before the public meeting could take place a second meeting of the subscribers to the Exeter & Crediton Navigation, as it had become known, was held at the *London Inn,* Exeter, on 26 January. A plan of the proposed route prepared by Thomas Gray, Surveyor to Exeter city chamber, was produced for inspection. It was to run from Four Mills (close to the present Crediton railway station) and along the Creedy valley to Cowley bridge, then partly by canal and partly along the River Exe to the public quay below Exe bridge. Many landowners present signified their assent to the proposals and it was agreed that a London surveyor 'conversant in the Business of forming Canals' be asked to examine the plan and report upon the expense necessary to complete it.[4]

The public meeting at Crediton on 5 February 1793 had different ideas, considering that the plans for the Exeter & Crediton Navigation would 'be of inconceivable Prejudice to the Public at large'. Those present, described as 'a numerous assemblage of gentlemen, clergy and other respectable inhabitants of Devon, and the adjacent counties', resolved that a canal from Topsham by way of Exeter to Crediton should be extended towards Bow and North Tawton and be linked at Topsham (or some more convenient place) with the proposed Grand Western Canal to Taunton. A committee was formed and subscription books opened for shares of £50, a maximum of ten and minimum of one being allotted to each subscriber. The demand was great, with 142 persons subscribing £67,600, a deposit of half a guinea (52½p) being payable at the time of application. It was reported that the amount subscribed would have been doubled had the books remained open for a further hour.

Christopher Hamlyn, who had been appointed treasurer, and his fellow committee members then retired to prepare an address to Sir Stafford Henry Northcote, Bt., of Upton Pyne, James Buller, M.P., John Quicke of Newton St Cyres, and other landowners concerned with the Exeter & Crediton Navigation. In this address, which was unanimously approved by the meeting, they set out their reasons for disapproval of the rival scheme.

The main point was that the navigation was too short. By commencing it at Exeter there would be delay and heavy expense for goods, as these would first have to pass through the Exeter Canal. Similarly, in terminating at Crediton, it would only be taken four miles into the countryside and so not answer its intended purpose. The projected Grand Western Canal from Topsham to Taunton offered new openings for trade which would not be possible if the navigation was cut as planned. The landowners were asked to withdraw their support from the Exeter & Crediton Navigation 'in favor of Justice and the Good of the Public'.[5]

The Exeter & Crediton subscribers had planned to meet again on 9 February. However, as the result of the feelings expressed at the Crediton meeting, there was no longer a need to keep up the pretence that it was a public concern and so the meeting was advertised as having been adjourned. The new committee for the rival canal from Topsham to Bow and North Tawton did meet on 12 February at the *Angel Inn,* Crediton, and resolved that it be called the Public Devonshire Canal. It was decided to employ a surveyor for a route from Topsham via Exeter to Crediton, North Tawton, Chumleigh and Barnstaple, and from North Tawton to Okehampton, Torrington and Bideford.[6]

A reply to the address from the Public Devonshire Canal committee was received from Sir Stafford Henry Northcote, Bt., James Buller, M.P., and John Quicke. They claimed that many of the arguments advanced to them were ill-founded, inferring that public opinion had been consulted before the plans for the Exeter & Crediton Navigation had been made. They considered that the real interest of those concerned with the Public Devonshire Canal was 'a struggle only to wrest the Concern out of the hands of private individuals'.

At the next committee meeting, on 21 February, Christopher Hamlyn enlightened those present about the supposed consultation with the public by the promoters of the Exeter & Crediton Navigation. Apparently a room had been booked in Exeter in the name of Pinhay & Co., the gentlemen attending having declared that they were on private business. This business was, in fact, the promotion meeting of the Exeter & Crediton Navigation. With a meeting held in such secrecy and with only 22 subscribers, including the three landowners already mentioned, plus John Pinhay and Richard Chamberlain, it could hardly be claimed to be for the public good. He pointed out that Richard Chamberlain had also been present at the Public Devonshire Canal meeting of 5 February, when approval had been given to that scheme. Christopher Hamlyn then returned to the theme that the Public Devonshire Canal was promoted for the public good, stressing that 'The Publick are not often, never Long Deceived; Their True Interest cannot long be concealed'.[7]

Although a reply was sent to the three landowners, the nature of this is unknown. The committee were adamant that the Public Devonshire Canal proposals should continue, resolving:

> That having embarked in the Cause of the Public, we will not desert it, but by every Act which our united Exertions can produce, endeavour to promote and secure, in the Execution of this Plan, the public Good.[8]

Events now moved quickly. On 18 February a meeting at Tavistock discussed the possibility of cutting a canal from the River Tamar to connect with the Public Devonshire Canal. The idea appeared to be feasible, and subscriptions were made towards the project. A further meeting for the promotion of the Tamar Canal, as the scheme became known, was held at the Market House, Tavistock, on 12 March. Proposals were agreed for a route from the navigable Tamar via Tavistock to Okehampton, with links to Launceston and Hatherleigh. A deputation from the Public Devonshire Canal attended this second meeting and offered co-operation in any scheme to link the two canals. This offer was

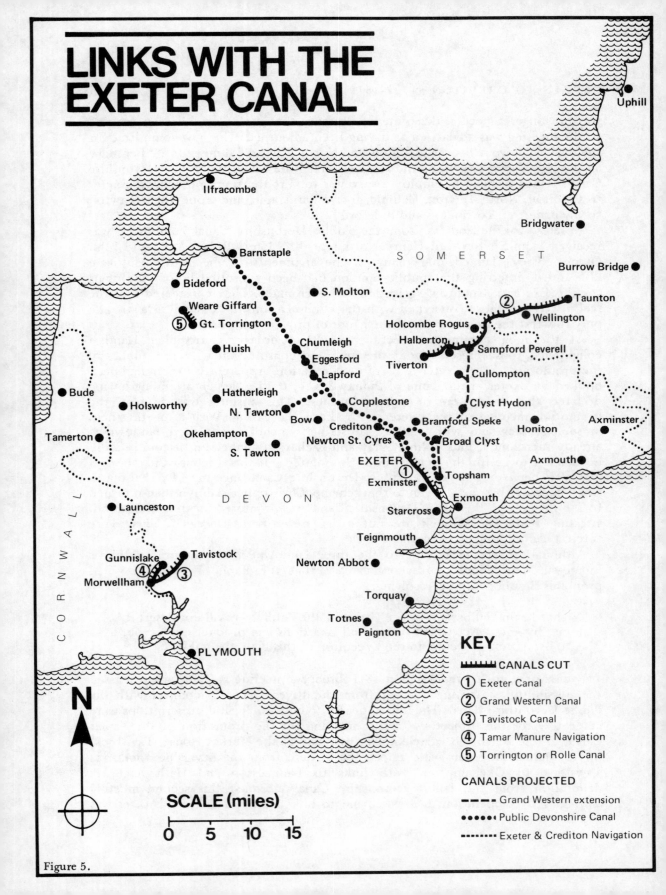

LINKS WITH THE EXETER CANAL

Uphill

Bridgwater

Burrow Bridge

S O M E R S E T

Ilfracombe

Barnstaple

Bideford

Weare Giffard

⑤ Gt. Torrington

S. Molton

Taunton

② Wellington

Holcombe Rogus

Halberton

Sampford Peverell

Chumleigh

Huish

Eggesford

Lapford

Tiverton

Cullompton

Bude

Holsworthy

Hatherleigh

N. Tawton

Bow

Copplestone

Clyst Hydon

Axminster

Crediton

Bramford Speke

Honiton

Tamerton

Okehampton

S. Tawton

Newton St. Cyres

Broad Clyst

Axmouth

EXETER

D E V O N

①

Exminster

Topsham

Launceston

Exmouth

Starcross

Teignmouth

Gunnislake

④

③ Tavistock

Newton Abbot

Morwellham

C O R N W A L L

Torquay

Totnes

Paignton

PLYMOUTH

KEY

⊢⊢⊢⊢ CANALS CUT

① Exeter Canal
② Grand Western Canal
③ Tavistock Canal
④ Tamar Manure Navigation
⑤ Torrington or Rolle Canal

CANALS PROJECTED

– – – Grand Western extension
•••••• Public Devonshire Canal
········ Exeter & Crediton Navigation

N

SCALE (miles)

0   5   10   15

Figure 5.

readily accepted, and of the 21 committee men elected at that meeting no fewer than five were also on the committee of the Public Devonshire Canal. By the close of the Tamar Canal promotion meeting £156,200 had been subscribed for shares of £50 value by 312 people. A call of half a guinea was made on each share at the time of application.[9]

A survey of the proposed route was undertaken by Thomas Bolton, surveyor, and George Bentley, engineer, but the line to Tavistock and Okehampton was never built. However, an Act of 1796 authorised the building of another canal from ˙Morwhellham quay to Tamerton bridge, a distance of 22 miles, with a branch to Launceston, so that a link could be made with the inland terminals of the proposed Bude Canal. All that was cut was 2¾ miles from Morwhellham to Newbridge, near Gunnislake. This, the Tamar Manure Navigation, survived until about 1929 when it became unnavigable. (The Inland Waterways Association [South-West Region] tried unsuccessfully to restore it between 1979–81.) A Tavistock canal, from Morwellham to Tavistock, was promoted in 1803 and opened in 1817. It had ceased working by the end of the century.[10]

On 26 March 1793, Bolton and Bentley attended a committee meeting of the Public Devonshire Canal and it was resolved that they should begin a survey of the intended line 'with all possible dispatch'. Their first report was made on 23 April, others following in May and June, and the final report was delivered on 30 July. Robert Whitworth was then asked to comment on the survey, and in September reported that it was satisfactory apart from a few minor alterations.[11]

To report progress to the subscribers to the Public Devonshire Canal a further meeting was held at the *Ship Inn*, Crediton, on 17 October 1793. The survey was explained in detail, plans being for a main line from Topsham to Barnstaple, a distance of 52 miles. From Topsham it would rise 287 feet to the summit level at Copplestone by way of Broad Clyst, Brampford Speke and Newton St Cyres, and then follow the Yeo valley towards the summit. The 3-miles-long summit level began at Copplestone, the line then falling 312 feet in its course along the Taw valley to Barnstaple. Two branches were planned, one 3½ miles long leaving the main line near Brampford Speke and going via Cowley Bridge and Exwick (where it crossed the River Exe) to Exeter. The other branch, 8 miles long, left the main line at Down St Mary, near Copplestone, terminating at North Tawton. The difference in figures for the rise and fall to and from the summit level is accounted for by the fact that the deposited plans do not show any connection with the River Exe at Topsham or the Grand Western Canal, nor with the River Taw at Barnstaple.[12]

The cost of construction was estimated to be £164,128 for the main line, with a further £11,000 for the Exeter branch and £22,000 for the North Tawton one. More money was needed to meet construction costs, the meeting deciding that 'a further Subscription be entered into, to be open to all persons who may chose to subscribe'. Furthermore, a call of 10s. 6d. was to be immediately paid on all existing shares. Interest at the rate of 5 per cent. per annum would be paid on all sums advanced until the work was completed, when it was forecast that an income of at least £11,650 per annum could be expected from tolls.[13]

The printed report of this meeting mentioned some of the goods expected to be carried on the canal. They included lime for manure, corn for export, Irish wool and yarn for the manufacture of woollen goods, stone and slate, cider, clay for the Staffordshire potteries, timber, coal and sea sand. The completion of the Grand Western Canal was expected to bring an additional trade for the Public Devonshire Canal in wool, hops, hardware, salt, glass, pottery, spirits, groceries, linen, etc. It also considered the possibilities of cutting yet another branch line to run to South Molton, which lay within five miles of the main line.

Having explained the plans for the Public Devonshire Canal in some detail the chairman, Christopher Hamlyn, then spoke about the rival Exeter & Crediton Navigation:

> . . . I hoped your Committee would have been enabled to state to you the probability of some accommodation with the party in opposition to us. But it seems the Report could not be completed sooner and your opponents as yet Retain their First Intention.
> I, for one, do not yet despair that by pursuing a Steady, Temperate Conduct arrangements may take place so as to procure what I conceive a most desirable consummation, a coalition of all parties concerned.[14]

Another general meeting of the subscribers took place at the now familiar venue, the *Ship Inn,* Crediton, on 7 November. Christopher Hamlyn once again acted as chairman, the purpose of the meeting being to raise further subscriptions for the undertaking. It was mentioned that the corporation and people of Barnstaple had given their approval to the canal and that many subscriptions had come from that district. The mayor of Barnstaple and three of his townsfolk were voted onto the committee, to represent the interests of their own area.[15]

Additional support came from the town of Bideford on 21 November when the mayor, corporation and principal inhabitants met at the Bridge Hall in the town, to consider the promotion of a canal from Bideford to connect with the Public Devonshire Canal. The proposal was agreed to and a committee formed whose numbers included the mayor, William Bickford Jackson. This committee was asked to contact Christopher Hamlyn to discuss the proposals and to gain information. Thomas Smith, town clerk of Bideford, was appointed secretary to the project.[16]

About this time a meeting was advertised to take place at the *Globe Inn,* Great Torrington, on 30 November to give consideration to the cutting of a canal 'from some navigable part of the River Torridge, above Bideford Bridge, to, or near to, the Town of Great Torrington'. The meeting took place as advertised with Denys Rolle, one of the principal landowners, acting as chairman. Also present were some of the committee appointed by the Bideford meeting a few days earlier, and nine of their number, including the mayor and town clerk of Bideford, were appointed to the committee of this new scheme. Probably to take account of the views of the Bideford meeting, the scheme now changed to a canal from Bideford to South Tawton with a branch to Great Torrington. This still gave the opportunity of a link with the Public Devonshire Canal and, possibly, also with the Bude Canal, a preliminary survey for the latter having already been undertaken by Bolton and Bentley. It was resolved to make a survey and open subscription books for the new scheme.[17]

On Saturday, 5 April 1794, the subscribers to the scheme, now entitled the 'Bideford, Torrington & Okehampton Canal', met again at Great Torrington. The chairman, Denys Rolle, had at his own expense arranged for a survey, plans and estimates of the proposed route to be made by George Bentley, aided on this occasion by a new surveyor, a Mr. Tozer. These were produced and approved:

> . . . but a sufficient Sum not having been subscribed to carry the Plan into Execution, *Resolved* that Subscriptions continue to be received at the Bideford Bank, Bideford, and the Offices of Messrs. Glubb and Tanner, Great Torrington and Barnstaple, the Solicitors to this Undertaking.[18]

The additional cash required was never to be subscribed. The canal mania was coming to an end and the inflationary effects of the Napoleonic Wars were already beginning to bite. The chairman of the Bideford, Torrington & Okehampton Canal project, Denys Rolle, died in 1797 and the scheme must have been abandoned by this time. An abortive attempt at a revival was made in 1810 when James Green, Surveyor of Bridges and Buildings for the County of Devon, prepared a plan for a Torridge Canal from Landcross, near Bideford, to Great Torrington. No further progress was made, apart from the publication of a parliamentary notice to announce the intention to apply for an Act. John, Lord Rolle, son of the late Denys Rolle, made a further and more successful attempt for a canal from Bideford to Great Torrington and work began on this project in 1823. He carried out the work at his own expense without an initial Act, employing James Green as engineer. The Torrington or Rolle Canal was completed and opened to traffic in February 1827. It closed in 1871, part of its route being used for a railway line between Bideford and Torrington.[19]

The Public Devonshire Canal was not without its troubles. These arose in winter 1793-94 when Robert Whitworth found that his recommendations on Bolton and Bentley's survey were not being adopted. Instead they were minutely investigated and objected to by the surveyor and engineer. It is strange that they should have taken this course of action, especially as Whitworth had few comments to make on their original survey.

However, in attempting to prove the superior nature of their own survey, Bolton and Bentley overplayed their hand. The point in question concerned the cutting of a mile of the canal on the branch to Exeter. Whitworth had suggested utilising the course of the mill stream that formerly fed Duryard Mills, estimating that the cost of adaptation would be £860. Bolton and Bentley thought otherwise, considering the cost to be £1,231 if Whitworth's recommendation was followed, or only £972 if their own plan of cutting a new channel was followed. The fallacy of cutting a mile of new deep channel through difficult ground, including the provision of two accommodation bridges and two road

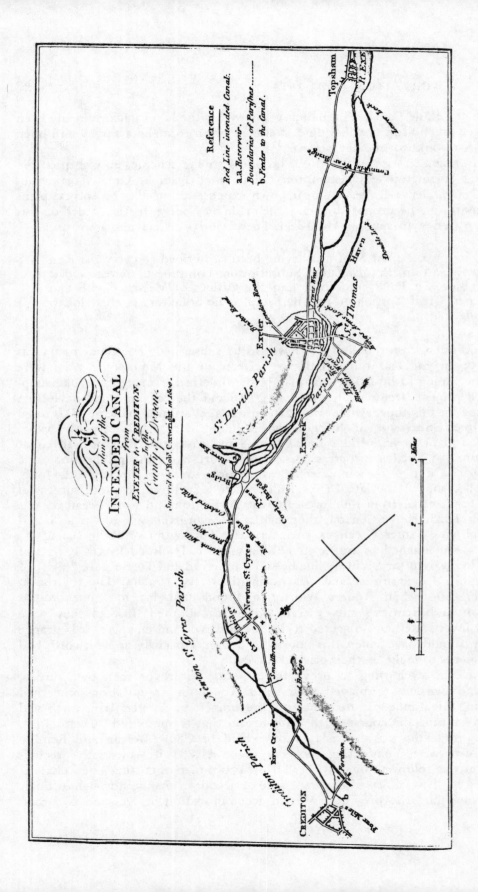

Figure 6. Plan of the Exeter and Crediton Navigation

bridges, for only £972 was easily exposed as the true cost was reckoned to be over £3,500.

Whitworth, who had been sent a copy of Bolton and Bentley's comments, wrote:

> . . . I am really sorry to find that you are in worse hands than I expected. When I was in your country if I had known I should have been contradicted in the manner I have been, by an artfull Man without any experience in the Business you would never have seen me there.[20]

Matters came to a head soon afterwards; a meeting being held at the *Angel Inn,* Crediton, on 11 February 1794 to try to resolve the differing opinions of the two engineers. In reference to the lower costs estimated by Bentley for the new channel at Duryard Mills, comment was made:

> . . . This Deception, unless proved to have arisen from Mistake, assuredly Merits severe Censure and leads to an alarming Jealousy of his other Calculations being founded on Erroneous Data however specious they may now Appear.

Bentley, having delivered his survey some six months earlier, now tried to justify his figures by stating that when an accurate survey was made the committee would find that the difference between his and Robert Whitworth's figures would disappear.

The committee thought otherwise, considering that these remarks justified Whitworth's figures. Bolton and Bentley had offered that the two sets of plans be examined by an independent engineer and if his decision was in favour of Whitworth they would meet the costs involved in the revision of the plans. If, however, the decision went in their favour the costs should be met by the Public Devonshire Canal committee. This offer was unanimously accepted, the committee deciding that the balance of Bolton and Bentley's account be retained as security.[21]

The name of the engineer who acted as mediator in the dispute is unknown. It seems that Whitworth was vindicated for, at a committee meeting held at the *Bear Inn,* Exeter, on 18 December 1794, the report of a select committee appointed to inspect Bolton and Bentley's charges for their survey of July 1793 was read and approved. Significantly, it was resolved that the accounts be prepared 'in Readiness for being laid before the Subscribers at a General Meeting' to be held as soon as possible. This was to be called for 'taking into its Consideration the further Steps necessary to be adopted in the Prosecution of the Scheme'. As many lived a considerable distance away it was agreed to postpone the meeting until after February, giving three weeks' advance notice of the date in the local newspapers.[22]

There is no record that the proposed meeting took place, nor of the subsequent exploits of Bolton and Bentley. There was a brief revival of the scheme in autumn 1800, following publication of a notice that the Exeter & Crediton Navigation intended to apply for an Act in the next session of parliament. The Public

Devonshire Canal committee met at the *Angel Inn*, Crediton, on 16 October of
that year to discuss the development. They decided to call a general meeting of
all subscribers on 13 November to seek their directions. Nothing appears to have
happened and the scheme slumbered.[23]

A final attempt at revival occurred in 1824, when the Torrington or Rolle
Canal was being cut, a newspaper reporting:

> A Canal is in contemplation from Wear Gifford, about three miles above
> Bideford, to go by Torrington, to Huish, the seat of Lord Clinton;
> proceed to Eggesford, the residence of the Hon. Newton Fellowes; and
> thence by Exeter to Topsham.

Nothing came of this scheme.[24]

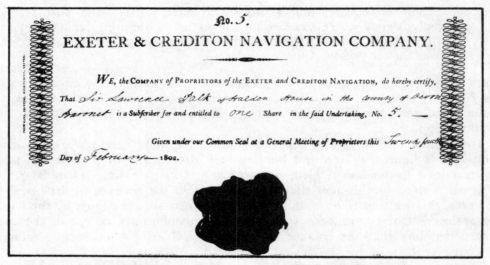

Figure 7. Exeter & Crediton Navigation share certificate

The Exeter & Crediton Navigation line was surveyed by Robert Cartwright in
1800 (*see* p. 28), and on 20 June 1801

> An Act for improving and extending the Navigation of the River Exe,
> from the public Quay at Exeter, to the public Road adjoining Four
> Mills, near Crediton, in the county of Devon, by making a navigable
> Canal or Cuts, and deepening and widening such parts of the Rivers
> Exe and Creedy, as shall be necessary for that Purpose . . .

received the Royal Assent. It gave powers to raise £21,400 by shares of £100
each, and an additional sum of £10,700 should this be necessary. The proprietors
were few in number, as might be expected of this secretive concern, and only
22 were named in the Act.[25]

The route authorised was the one originally proposed in 1793. The junction with the River Exe, above Exe bridge, was planned to have a lock. This would give entrance to a basin with the usual wharf facilities such as warehouses, cranes, etc., the navigation then rejoining the river above Head Wear. It would leave the river once more near Exwick and then follow the Creedy valley to Crediton, using that river for part of its route. A spacious basin was also planned for the terminal point at Crediton.

Very heavy rates of toll were allowed by the Act. These, per ton per mile, were 1s. 0d. for timber; 6d. for all other goods except limestone, manure or lime for manure; 2d. for limestone and manure; and 1½d. per hogshead for lime used for manure. An additional duty of up to 2d. per ton was payable by craft using the basins belonging to the navigation. The Act also made specific reference that the rights of the mayor and city chamber of Exeter and of the management of the Exeter Canal were to remain unaltered.

A general meeting of the proprietors of the Exeter & Crediton Navigation was held on 24 February 1802 at which shares were issued to subscribers. Shares nos. 1 to 5 (*see* opposite) went to Sir Lawrence Palk, Bt., of Haldon House. The city chamber also subscribed to this issue, considering that the new navigation would bring more traffic to their own canal. Nothing happened until 1808 when committee meetings were held and a call of £10 made on each share to buy land. A book published in that year noted:

> This work is now complete as far as Exweek, but under the present arrangement, no very sanguine expectations are generally entertained of its being shortly accomplished with a favourable issue. [26]

A further call of £10 per share was made at the committee meeting held on 26 July 1809. James Green, the engineer to the Exeter & Crediton Navigation, advertised for 100 canal cutters between June and August 1811, some land having been purchased or leased the previous year. A further call of £1 per share was made in July 1812 and after 1813 news of the undertaking disappeared from the columns of the local newspapers. According to Moore, the Devon historian:

> Soon after procuring this Act, the work was commenced just above the city. When about half a mile only was completed, however, owing to a variety of unforseen difficulties and expenses, the proceedings were suspended and finally abandoned.

In fact, in September 1818 the clerk to the Exeter & Crediton Navigation wrote to the navigation committee of the Exeter Canal to say that his proprietors had resolved to abandon their canal. Following the abandonment, the next year or so was spent in disposing of the unwanted land. [27]

And so the plans of the Exeter & Crediton Navigation proprietors came to an end, to be forgotten by all but a few until 1973. Then a remarkable discovery was made. In May of that year contractors excavating a flood relief channel for the River Exe discovered a large amount of brickwork about 10 feet below ground level, just upstream of Exe Bridge North. Exeter Industrial Archaeology Group were contacted and visited the site, and construction was halted for one week whilst they conducted a thorough survey. This showed that the brickwork was the remains of a lock about 80ft. long and 14ft. wide. It had been designed for double gates, yet nowhere were the side walls more than seven courses high, giving an indication that work had begun on the lock but possibly never completed.[28]

The Exeter & Crediton Navigation abandonment came shortly before great improvements took place on the adjacent Exeter Canal, the same engineer, James Green, being involved with both waterways.

Chapter Four

ALTERATIONS AND EXTENSIONS (1820–1830)

JAMES GREEN'S REPORT 'for bettering the navigation' was ready for the navigation committee by October 1820. It showed that the Exeter Canal was in a very bad state of repair, as also was the channel leading from the Exe estuary to Lower sluice. This channel was narrow and tortuous, with banks of soft mud, but no towing path. To avoid the shoals, most craft had pilotage from Topsham to the canal entrance.

He considered that the site for Lower sluice had been ill-chosen, because coastal craft were only able to enter the canal at spring tides. Consequently, many imported goods had to be unloaded at Topsham and sent overland to Exeter. Even when access to the canal was possible, the 2-miles-long pound between Lower sluice and Double locks was only usable at certain times. The reason was that it was emptied at low tides to allow drainage of the meadow lands which adjoined the canal. Craft of 9-ft. draught, the largest that could navigate to Exeter quay, could only pass this length when sufficient water had been drawn off from the upper pound to make progress possible.

The upper pound from Double locks to King's Arm sluice was in need of dredging, because the depth of water was only 8 feet in many places. King's Arm sluice, too, suffered through only having one pair of gates as craft could not pass through to the River Exe in times of flood and were often delayed for days. Though the river between King's Arm sluice and Trew's weir formed a fine basin, it also suffered from silting and a uniform depth could only be maintained by constant dredging, causing great expense. Green was also critical of the masonry at the Lower sluice, noting that it was 'greatly dilapidated'. The single gates, newly fitted in 1819, were said to be 'of a very imperfect construction'. The masonry of Double locks was also in a bad state and the canal banks and towing path needed repair.

He recommended that Lower sluice be rebuilt as a conventional pound lock with two pairs of gates, the sill of the lower pair (the seaward end) to be relaid at a reduced level equivalent to the height of the shoal opposite Topsham. This would ensure that craft able to pass that shoal would be certain to gain entry to the canal. For easier navigation he proposed that the pound from Lower sluice to Double locks should have a uniform depth of 10 feet. When Double locks was under repair he suggested that the sill of the lower gates should also be relaid at a lower level (when new gates were being fitted) as this would help to reduce the water pressure on the gates at Lower sluice. The former drainage functions of this pound were to be undertaken by a separate channel leading to the tideway. The new channel would be cut on the west side of the canal banks or, alternatively, the water could be carried through pipes under the canal and discharged into the Exe estuary at some intermediate point. Other proposals included straightening the pound from Double locks to King's Arms sluice and dredging it to a depth of 10 feet, and dredging to a similar depth at the river basin in Exeter.

As an alternative to these improvements, which would cause a long interruption in the trade of the canal, Green suggested that a new Lower sluice with two pairs of gates could be built further down the tidal channel. A new cut would be made from the head of this sluice to a point in the canal above the present Lower sluice, having a basin 'capable of containing several vessels'. The construction work for the extension could be carried out without interference with navigation and have the additional advantage that, with the canal entrance nearer to the Exe estuary, many of the bends and shoals currently encountered would be avoided.[1]

The city chamber had to sanction any improvements and repairs considered necessary by the navigation committee. The latter had been informed of the perilous state of Double locks and its gates, for 'without the greatest Attention immediate Danger may be apprehended of their total destruction'. Approval was given for repairs to Double locks and for the dredging and straightening of the upper part of the canal. James Green estimated that the lock repairs would not exceed £400, an additional £200 being required for making new gates.[2]

The repairs took far longer than anticipated and it was not until February 1822 that the navigation committee was able to report 'the late extensive repairs on the Canal are nearly completed, the canal having been opened for all vessels soon after Christmas'. The reasons for the delay were manifold, there being:

> . . . great regret that the Season should have proved so unfavourable which, with the unexpected ruinous state of the masonry and decay of the upper Gates at the Double Lock and Platform have undoubtedly occasioned a greater increased expense that was at first calculated on.[3]

The alterations had been completed at a time when the Exeter woollen industry was in a decline. The export trade in serge cloth had finished during the Napoleonic Wars and all that remained was a coastwise trade to London, with cloth destined for export by the East India Company. Much of this was shipped from Topsham, probably owing to the reluctance of 'foreign' coaster crews to use the canal in its poor navigational state. When the East India Company lost its monopoly in 1833 it sounded the death knell for Exeter's woollen trade.

Perhaps the most dramatic change in trade was that Exeter became primarily an importer, rather than an exporter as in former years. Admittedly some industries had grown up to take the place of the woollen trade, chiefly paper-making and tanning, but the main emphasis was now on imports. Coal was the chief import and rose from 30,944 tons in 1784 to 65,164 tons in 1818. The expansion was due to the increasing use of this fuel for domestic heating, aided by the construction of a gas works near the quay in 1816.[4]

Because the alterations in 1820–22 had failed to improve the tidal channel below the Lower sluice, nor make improvements to the sluice itself, there were many complaints about delays and inconvenience, notably from the merchants of Exeter. James Green was asked to make surveys of the practicability of extending the canal further into the Exe estuary. In his report of 1 March 1824 he recommended that the line be continued to Turf, two miles beyond the Lower sluice, as craft of 12-ft. draught could navigate to this point at all times. He noted that there were two possible routes for this extension, either on an almost straight line through valuable enclosed marshlands, or by keeping close to the river and so passing through marshland of little worth. The first route would require many bridges to connect the two halves of divided property, whilst the latter would only need one bridge.[5]

In June 1824 the mayor of Exeter and three of his colleagues visited Sir Lawrence Palk, Bt., of Haldon House, a shareholder in the abortive Exeter & Crediton Navigation. Their purpose was 'to ascertain upon what terms' he would permit the extension of the canal to pass through his property. Sir Lawrence agreed to the plans, saying that he would make no charge. However, before giving his formal consent, he wanted to know that Sir John Acland of Killerton, the other landowner concerned, also approved of the extension. Later Sir John's steward called upon the mayor, examined the plans and remarked that there could be 'no possible Objection to the adoption of a Measure so beneficial to Sir John Acland's property'. Sir John thought otherwise, writing to express his reservations and to ask for compensation for any land taken.[6]

The mayor then asked Thomas Telford, the eminent canal engineer, to examine the whole of the Exeter Canal and the various plans suggested by James Green for its improvement and extension to Turf. Telford's report of 31 July 1824 basically agreed with Green's recommendations, suggesting that the King's Arms sluice be rebuilt as a conventional pound lock with two pairs of gates. He also considered it to be 'absolutely necessary' to construct a conventional lock at the seaward end of the canal. He approved the plans for the line of the extension to Turf, which ran close to the Exe estuary, concluding:

> . . . the outer line of extension, as laid down in Mr. Green's plan ought to be adopted, without variation; and I am convinced, that if the works are executed in a perfect manner, under his directions, that the improvements will be found a very valuable acquisition . . .[7]

Telford's report was presented to the navigation committee on 4 August 1824, a day on which he accompanied the mayor and receiver of Exeter along the canal banks to view the proposed alterations. On 21 February 1825 the city chamber confirmed the recommendation for the extension to Turf according to Green's plans, as approved by Telford. The navigation committee were then empowered 'to make such contracts and give such directions' as thought necessary to carry the plans into effect. At the same meeting the finance committee was authorised to borrow £12,000 to pay for the construction costs. On 20 April Mr. Crockett, a member of the city chamber, was asked to act as treasurer and the £12,000 was paid over to him. This sum was part of a total of £15,000, the estimated cost of the extension, and was raised by a mortgage of the canal and Exe island to a Mr. Cresswell. The money was soon to be needed, as the first sod was cut that very day.[8]

There were also problems, dating back to 1820, with money at the quay. In November of that year the books of the wharfinger, Thomas Upham, were 'considerably in Arrear'. It was admitted on that occasion there were grounds for excuse because 'the Wharfinger has not had the Assistance which is considered necessary'. When the accounts were examined in April 1821 there was a further deficiency of £2,451, plus interest of £254 to Lady Day, this being money owed by traders using the canal. A Mr. Strong was paid 60 guineas for 'his great trouble in arranging and settling the Wharfinger's Account'.

Regrettably, in December 1824 the wharfinger's accounts were once more in arrears, this time for £1,739. Upham was immediately suspended from duty and the books, papers and cash he held were impounded. He subsequently attended a meeting of the navigation committee but was unable to offer any explanation for the deficit. A request for the payment of his salary to the date of suspension was refused, the committee considering that this 'should be carried to the Credit of his Account'.

Mr. Strong was again called in to examine the book and found that, according to the arrears book, the deficiency was £1,739, whilst by the receipts book it was £2,060. The committee decided that the latter sum was due from Upham, who was then discharged from his office. A few days later he wrote asking to examine the books and papers. Permission was granted on condition that they were not removed from the office and that a clerk should be present throughout the examination. Upham also queried the amount of the deficiency and was told that unless he could prove it was incorrect the full arrears must be settled by Lady Day 1825. As payment was not made by the appointed date the navigation committee decided to prosecute him for 'several lots of Embezzlement whilst in Office'. In June, Upham wrote again and proposed paying £600 in discharge of his liabilities, the committee recommending that the city chamber 'do accept that sum in full of their claim'.[9]

There was a happy ending to this squalid affair for the man who had coped with Upham's work during his suspension. Although Mr. Strong had nominally been wharfinger throughout that period, Richard Banfill, one of the clerks, had to manage the day-to-day business. In recompense, the navigation committee voted him a gratuity of £20 for 'his extraordinary labours' from the time of Upham's dismissal until the appointment of a new wharfinger, Mr. Campion, at a salary of £150 per annum. By November 1825 there were more problems, this time from vandalism, as 'great damage has lately been done to King's Arms sluice by breaking the Locks and injuring the Gates'. A reward of £5 was offered on the conviction of the offenders, with a similar amount for the detection of any further vandalism.[10]

Although the city chamber had requested monthly reports on the progress of the extension to Turf, the navigation committee do not appear to have taken any action on this request. Almost a year passed before James Green made a report, dated 24 March 1826, in which he set out some of the difficulties encountered and made further recommendations.

Since his earlier report of March 1824 storms had made breaches in the natural sea wall formed by Dawlish Warren. This had caused some extraordinary high tides in new places, particularly in 1824 when the whole of the marshlands intended for the extension was flooded. Much of the route was carried across land flooded by the sea at every tide and, though between 200 and 300 labourers were at work, it was difficult to build and maintain the embankments to the required height. In any event, these had shown to be insufficient to prevent flooding at extra high tides and he therefore recommended that they should be raised another three feet. If the banks of the existing canal were also raised to the same height it would allow a 15-ft. depth for navigation between Turf and Double locks.

He also suggested that the bed of the canal from Double locks to King's Arms sluice be deepened to allow craft with a 14-ft. draught. As the final portion of the waterway between King's Arms sluice and the quay would be difficult and expensive to alter, the bed being solid sandstone, Green proposed making a new canal basin on the west side of the river. This would be entered through a cut made below King's Arm sluice and allow craft to enter or leave the 'floating harbour' at any state of the tide and remain undisturbed when the River Exe was in flood.[11]

Again the city chamber sought independent advice, once more turning to Thomas Telford for his comments. Telford agreed wholeheartedly with James Green's suggestions, writing:

> . . . It appears to me, that making the canal 15 feet, instead of 12 feet of water, will admit a class of vessels, which will greatly promote the prosperity of the port, and promise more than will compensate for the additional expense . . .
> The works now in hand, are proper in their principle, and are, in my opinion, conducted in a manner which does credit to those concerned, and will, I have no doubt, answer the intended purpose.[12]

Telford had come to Exeter to inspect the work in progress on the extension whilst preparing his report and the navigation committee made use of his advice on other matters. He thought that a further £6,000 would be required to complete the canal and agreed that Green's estimate of £10,000 made ample provision for the new canal basin at Exeter.

Arrangements were subsequently made for the city chamber to borrow £10,000 from the Exchequer Bill Loan Commissioners to finance the cost of the basin. The loan was granted in 1827, security being given by a mortgage on the canal. The Commissioners' consulting engineer, whose advice was sought before the approval of any loan, was none other than Thomas Telford.

Meanwhile, construction costs were escalating. In December 1826 James Green prepared a long report for the navigation committee, showing the total expenditure to date and giving an estimate of the cost of completion. The total was £45,391, which included the purchase of land for the extension, the building of the new basin at Exeter, legal expenses, and his own fees. Much of the increase on the original estimates had been caused through unforeseen circumstances, such as flooding after the storm damage to Dawlish Warren.[13]

An example of the difficulties encountered is given in the construction of Turf lock. When excavations through the stiff alluvial clay had reached a depth of 20 feet below the surface of the marshes, a pile was driven in to try to find the level of hard foundations. All that happened was that water forced its way upwards around the pile and by the following morning the sides of the lock pit had sunk perpendicularly at least 10 feet, whilst the bottom of the pit had risen upwards by a similar amount. To overcome these problems the lock sides had to be timber-piled and then strengthened by transverse whole timbers. So that water pressure could not force up the invert of the lock, elm plank trunking was placed beneath the rubble masonry foundations. The masonry of the lock and the sea defences were then built in granite, the lock having dimensions of 122ft. by 29ft. (*see* p. 68 for a plan of the lock).[14]

It seems that the navigation committee were satisfied by James Green's report, yet failed to inform the city chamber of the great increase in costs. Oblivious of these details, the city chamber confirmed the committee's recommendation and approved the construction of the new basin at Exeter in May 1827. The work on the extension to Turf was now drawing to a close, one of the last acts being to block off the old sea entrance at Lower sluice before the new line was formally opened on Friday, 15 September 1827. The intention was that the schooner *Dispatch,* under command of Captain Thomas Barratt, should be the first to enter and use the canal. Unfortunately a strong north wind began to blow off the coast which, coupled with neap tides, left the schooner with insufficient water to proceed when still some distance from Turf lock. In consequence, a barge specially fitted up for the occasion with a band of musicians aboard was used by the mayor, members of the city chamber, navigation committee and their friends.

The ceremonial barge left Exeter quay at 9 a.m. A contemporary newspaper described the opening ceremonies:

> . . . a number of boats followed the barge, and the banks were lined with pedestrians. The music played popular airs, and in the distance was heard the deep and fine-toned Cathedral bells, harmonising sweetly with the silver-tongued peal in Exminster tower. The interest of the scene was not a little heightened by the circumstance of twelve vessels, and some of them of considerable bulk and tonnage, descending the Canal at the same time. On emerging from the old lock the approbation of the multitude, both on the water and on land, was testified at the altered and improved appearance of this part of the line by repeated cheers . . . Proceeding onwards, at three hours from leaving Exeter Quay, the barge reached the termination of the Canal, and here the sea-lock with its gates and numerous contrivances, were such as to

excite the admiration and astonishment of the spectators . . . On the arrival of the party, Capt. Barratt, who was much annoyed at the singular circumstance which had at such an interesting moment stuck his vessel fast, was making efforts to free her . . . The barge and boats having been admitted into the basin, the sea-gates were opened amidst the firing of cannon, sound of music, and deafening shouts from the numbers assembled to witness the ceremony, and the vessels passed through, and on their return were accompanied by the *Ranger* yacht, (being gaily dressed in honour of the day) several additional boats, loaded barges, &c., &c., and having partaken of a cold collation provided for the occasion, proceeded on their return to this city . . . At a quarter past 5 p.m. the party reached the Quay, where they landed under salutes of artillery and the loudest cheering.[15]

Later that day the navigation committee and some of their friends met for dinner at the *Royal Clarence Hotel,* Exeter. Congratulations on the success of the extension were abundant, with toasts drunk in profusion. James Green was almost forgotten, though he was allowed to explain why the work had taken longer than anticipated. On Saturday it was the turn of the men employed on the canal, who 'were plentifully regaled with beef and pudding, and strong beer' at Perriman's, Double locks. On Sunday the schooner *Dispatch* at last entered the canal and made her way to the basin by Turf lock. The following day the ceremonial barge was pressed into service again, taking a party of ladies and gentleman to Turf. Here they went aboard the *Dispatch* and 'quadrilles were danced, an elegant cold collation partaken of'. The banks were again crowded with spectators and, to the sound of cannon firing, a display of sky rockets and the blaze of bonfires, the craft returned to the quay that evening.[16]

Though the extension to Turf was now complete, navigation to the quay at Exeter was not possible by craft exceeding 9ft. 6in. draught. Work was still in hand on deepening the remaining sections and more money was required. In December 1827 the treasurer, Mr. Crockett, told the navigation committee that £40,337 had already been spent on the canal. Later that month the city chamber authorised the borrowing of a further £13,000. Some of this was needed to meet a new expense, the construction of a lock opposite Topsham and above the old Lower sluice. This came after litigation with Robert Davy of Topsham, from one of the ship-building families in that town. He built men-of-war for the navy and also East Indiamen and West Indiamen. Apart from ship-building, he also had interests in the coal, timber and limestone trades. Russell and Son of Exeter were also ship-builders and one of their craft, the 150-ton *London, of Inverness,* was built on the Haven banks near King's Arms sluice. She was launched in June 1827, the unusual name being based on the ports between which she was intended to trade.[17]

The basin at Exeter was at first planned to be 630ft. long. In July 1828 the navigation committee agreed with Green's recommendation to increase the length to 750 feet, though it was later to be extended to 917 feet. The width was finally settled at 110 feet, tapering to 90 feet at the entrance, and there was an overall depth of 18 feet.

From the start of work on the extension, money to finance construction costs had been borrowed on mortgage. The city chamber did not apply at the outset for an Act of Parliament for this purpose, being deterred by the costs involved. If they had done so they would probably have chosen the inland route for the extension. Despite the extra costs of having to build many bridges to link areas of valuable enclosed marshland and of acquiring the land, these could have been far less in the long term as the route was about a fourth shorter than the one selected. With hindsight the city chamber may well have wished that they had applied for an Act at the start of the new work because there were several slippages on the banks, the canal having been built on insecure foundations in places. The day of reckoning came when the navigation committee and the city chamber found their powers and finances were inadequate to deal with the alterations still in progress. In November 1828 leave was sought for a Bill to raise money for completing the canal.[18]

At this time the major work being undertaken was the deepening of the pound from Double locks to King's Arms sluice. It took longer than expected, owing to the need to cut through areas of solid rock, but was finally ready for craft of up to 200 tons burthen on Friday, 12 December 1828. To fill it quickly the gates of both Turf and Double locks were opened to let the tide in, the first time that the sea had flowed to Exeter for many centuries. When the tide turned the gates were closed and the canal 'topped up' by the River Exe through King's Arms sluice. Then came the usual celebrations for the labourers:

> The workmen, amounting to about two hundred, were regaled on the occasion with eatables, and drank success to the city of Exeter in good strong beer, and at intervals gave several hearty cheers, the men enjoying themselves around the blazing bonfires, which presented a truly picturesque appearance.

The practicalities of working the canal were not forgotten amidst the celebration. The treasurer, Mr. Crockett, was asked to form an establishment of men and horses for towing craft from Turf to Exeter, the rate to be from 5s. 0d. for each man and horse according to the tonnage.[19]

The Act 'for altering, extending; and improving the Exeter Canal' received the Royal Assent on 14 May 1829. It sanctioned the extension from Lower sluice to Turf, though this had already been completed, and authorised the construction of the new canal basin at Exeter. Following the litigation between Robert Davy and the city chamber, the Act also approved the construction of a new entrance, with a lock, opposite Topsham. Of more immediate importance were the powers to levy certain tolls and dues and to raise 'a competent sum of money' to complete the works by statutory mortgages of the canal, tolls and rates leviable under the Act.[20]

By the time the Act was passed the city chamber had spent £96,998 on the Exeter Canal works. Using the powers conferred upon them by legislation they borrowed a further £85,900. Part of this sum was spent in redeeming existing loans and mortgages and part in financing further construction costs. The amount was secured by 1,160 statutory mortgages of £50 or £100 each, these bearing interest at 5 per cent. per annum.[21]

Rules for the guidance of persons using the canal were agreed to in August 1829. Two months later James Green produced plans of the new lock at Topsham for inspection by the navigation committee. When built it would shorten the time taken by the Topsham traders to reach Exeter as, since the closure of Lower sluice, they had to go down river to Turf to enter the canal. Efforts by traders to get Lower sluice re-opened had resulted in the successful litigation by Robert Davy, but another three years were to elapse before the lock was completed.[22]

Meanwhile, work on the Exeter canal basin was continuing with great vigour. In summer 1830 operations were carried on night and day and the opening date was fixed for 29 September. The city chamber made arrangements for the ceremony, having their five large flat lighters fitted out with masts and awnings and then tastefully decorated with evergreens, flowers and flags. A further small barge, similarly decorated, was reserved exclusively for the band. The barges, with the mayor, city chamber and their invited guests aboard, were to be towed down the canal to Double locks and then to return, preceding the ships already waiting there. Needless to say, the customary cold collation was to be provided at Double locks.[23]

Wednesday, 29 September, was a fine day. The celebrations began at about 12.40 p.m. when the barges left for Double locks, saluted by the firing of cannon and the ringing of the cathedral bells. It was estimated that there were more than 13,000 people present to view the scene, many of them following the waterborne procession. On return to Exeter:

> . . . the usual ceremony of *Christening* was performed by the Mayor, and the Civic barge accompanied by the *Mary and Thomas* Schooner proceeded to the head of the Dock, when the ceremony being concluded, (at a quarter to three) the company dispersed apparently as highly gratified as it was possible for them to be. A general jollification then took place amongst the Navigators, sailors and others connected with the port . . .[24]

For the benefit of the navigators and their families the city chamber provided six hogsheads of beer, 200 half-quartern loaves and one cwt. of cheese and gave 200 pairs of red garters as a distinguishing badge. The mayor and city chamber were invited by some 200 of the principal inhabitants to attend a dinner at Congdon's Royal Subscription Rooms after the opening ceremony had been concluded. This function was to show the approval of the city at the completion of the canal basin and the assembled company sat down at 6 p.m. to a range of delicacies that included 60 quarts of turtle soup and six haunches of venison. Afterwards came the speeches and the toasts. The mayor, referring to the extension to Turf, produced a piece of paper which gave an estimate of about £6,000 for this work in about 1690. He was pleased that the city chamber had at last been able to carry out the ideas of their forefathers.[25]

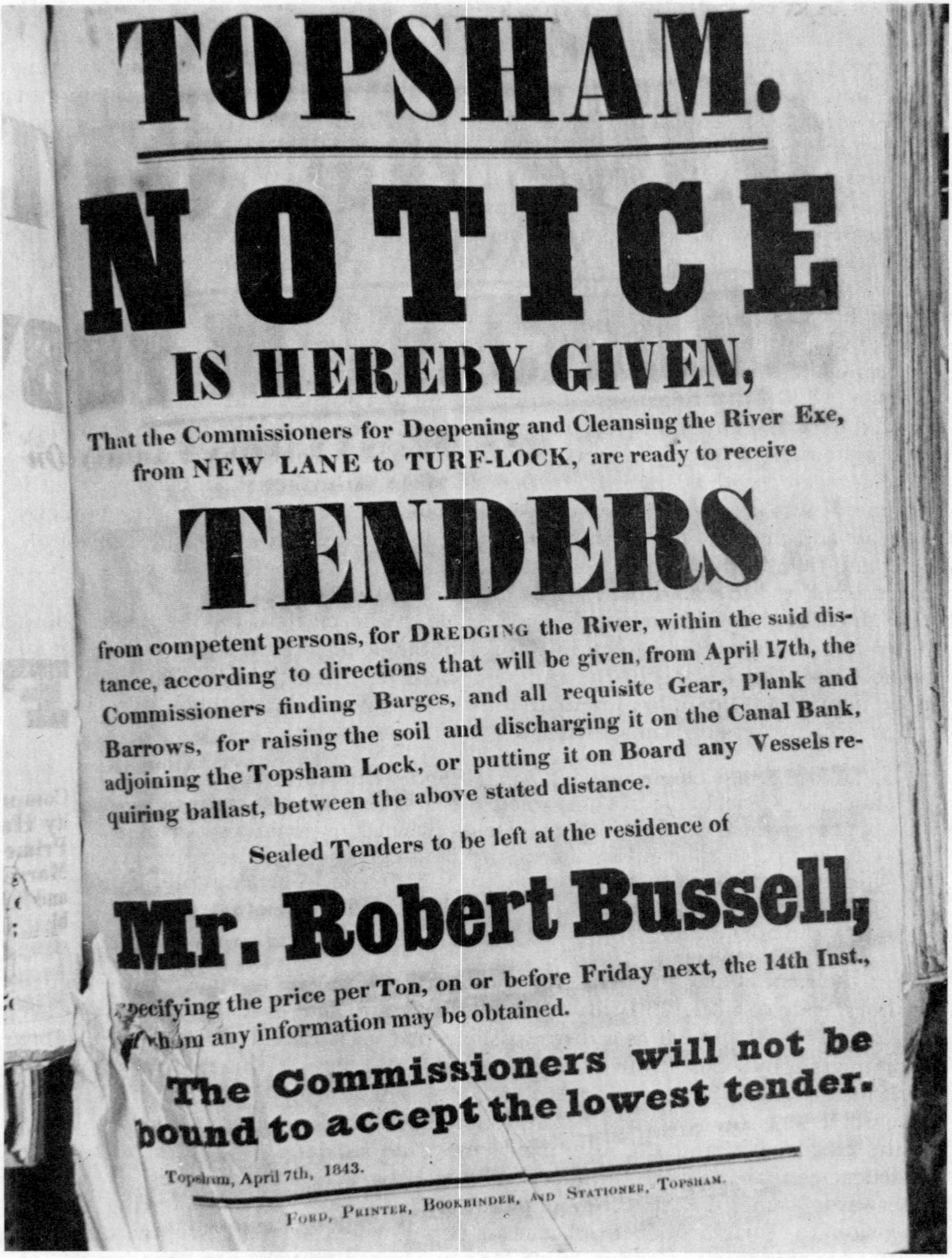

Figure 8. Notice seeking tenders for dredging the River Exe.

The diners toasted the Royal family, the mayor and the city of Exeter, the bishop and the clergy of the diocese, the lord-lieutenant of the county, the county members of Parliament, etc., and then, at the 17th toast they remembered the man who had made the day possible. James Green's health was drunk with acclaim and he was loudly cheered.

Within a few years the cheers were to change to recriminations, for the true costs of the alterations and extension were not yet known.

Passage Money including Steward's Fee to LONDON.

Cabin	- - -	£1 1s.
Deck	- - -	£0 10s.

Passage Money including Steward's Fee to COWES & PORTSMOUTH.

Cabin	- -	15s. 0d.
Deck	- - -	7s. 6d.

STEAM COMMUNICATION

BETWEEN

Topsham & London

CALLING AT COWES AND PORTSMOUTH.

THE PUBLIC ARE RESPECTFULLY INFORMED, THAT THE

STEAM PACKET,

ZEPHYR,

JAMES BEER, Commander,

WILL LEAVE TOPSHAM FOR LONDON, AS FOLLOWS:

JUNE. 4, 1842,	SATURDAY	1 o'clock.	afternoon	AUG. 6, 1842,	SATURDAY	5 o'clock,	evening
„ 12,	SUNDAY	8	morning	„ 13,	.....	12	noon
„ 18,	SATURDAY	1	afternoon	„ 20,	.....	5	evening
„ 25,	„	6	evening	„ 27,	.....	10	morning
JULY 2,	„	12	noon	SEP. 3,	.....	4	afternoon
„ 9,	„	7	evening	„ 10,	.....	11	morning
„ 16,	„	12	noon	„ 17,	.....	4	afternoon
„ 23,	„	12	noon	„ 24,	.....	9	morning
„ 30,	„	11	morning				

And leaves LONDON for TOPSHAM, every Wednesday Morning, at 8 o'Clock, calling at PORTSMOUTH on Thursday at 2 o'Clock, in the Afternoon.

For further particulars, apply to the St George Steam Packet Company's Office, Cathedral Yard, Exeter; or in London, at the Office, 137, Leadenhall Street, and St. George's Wharf, adjoining St. Katherine's Docks.

W. HOWELL, AGENT.

Figure 9.   Sailing bill of steam packet *Zephyr* from Topsham.

Chapter Five

MANAGED UNDER MORTGAGE (1831–1857)

WITH THE COMPLETION of the extension to Turf and the canal basin at Exeter, there was a great upsurge in trade and profits. Prior to 1827 all craft had been charged a toll of 5s. 6d., though in that year the tolls were revised and based on tonnage. The overall increase for the larger ships remained minimal because there was no longer a need for pilotage from the Exe estuary at Topsham to the canal entrance. Towage charges, too, were lower through the use of horses along the widened banks where men had previously done the towing (craft were forbidden to use the canal under sail to prevent damage to the banks). The enlarged dimensions enabled many coastal craft to carry their cargoes direct to Exeter, instead of having to unload into lighters, and the price of coal at the quay was halved.

The profits of Exeter quay increased rapidly in the period immediately following the opening of the canal. The following figures are based on two-year averages:

1830–31	..	£6,253
1832–33	..	£6,866
1834–35	..	£6,921
1836–37	..	£7,506
1838–39	..	£8,261
1840–41	..	£8,473
1842–43	..	£8,550[1]

Topsham lost much of its trade when the canal was extended to Turf, but the establishment of steamship services to London, France and the Channel Islands brought a new source of income. By the 1840s the steam packet *Zephyr* was leaving Topsham for London each Saturday, calling en route at Cowes and Portsmouth, and returning from the capital on Wednesday (*see* opposite). The city chamber showed that they were aware of the coming challenge of steam by supporting proposals for a railway from Exeter canal basin to Four Mills, Crediton, with a subscription of £1,000. An Act for this purpose was passed in 1832, but the powers lapsed without anything being done.[2]

In March 1832, whilst work continued on the new Topsham lock, the navigation committee authorised some additional comforts at the Custom House on the quay. W. Cornish was asked to erect a water closet for the use of 'Officers of the Establishment' at a cost not exceeding £25. In September of the same year modernisation was completed, Topsham lock being ready for use. As the Exe estuary below the lock was only suitable for craft of limited draught the lock dimensions were smaller than at Turf, being 88ft. long and 25ft. wide.[3]

The increase in trade at the newly-open canal basin meant a move for the chief clerk, Richard Banfill, then employed in the wharfinger's office on the quay. He was asked to occupy a house near the basin, to assist 'in general superintendence & management of the Trade and Vessels of the Canal' (*see* below). The accommodation must have been primitive; Banfill attended the next meeting of the navigation committee to plead the necessity of a kitchen and wash-house, to which they agreed. Earlier, the committee had approved an application to build warehouses at the basin, on a 60-year lease at a ground rent of £10 per annum.[4]

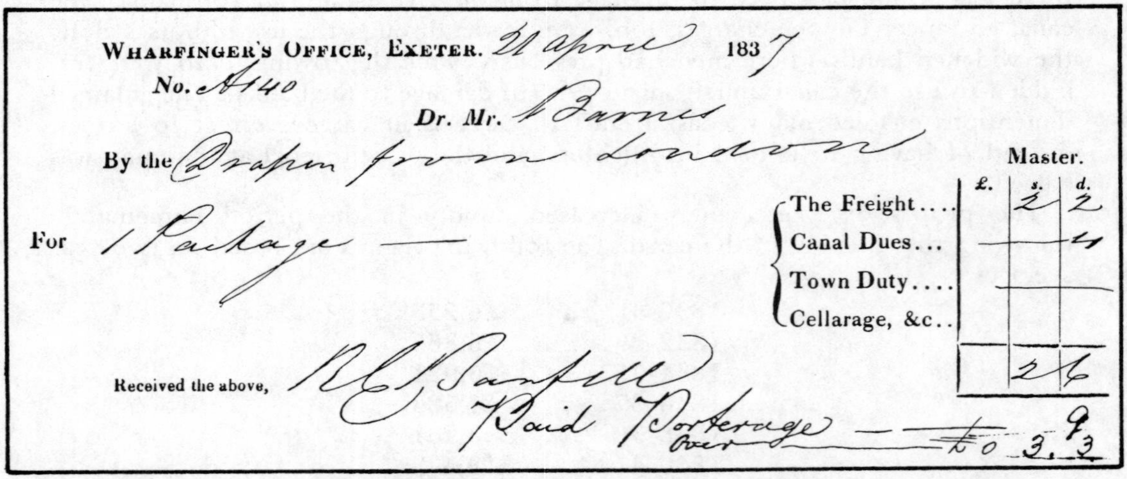
WHARFINGER'S OFFICE, EXETER. 21 April 1837

No. A140

Dr. Mr. Barnes

By the Draper from London Master.

For 1 Package —

	£.	s.	d.
The Freight....		2	2
Canal Dues...			4
Town Duty....			
Cellarage, &c..			
		2	6

Received the above, R C Banfill

Paid Porterage Over — £0 3.3

Figure 10. Wharfinger's receipt signed by Richard Banfill.

The city chamber may well have been pleased to think that their expenditure on improvements to the canal had at last come to an end, but they were soon to have a shock. In 1832 some unexpected bills were produced for labour and masonry work, dating back to the time that construction began. Up to April 1828 most of the labouring jobs had been done by a gang under the direction of James Chapman. Though it had been arranged that payment should be made for measured work, no settlement was made by the time of his death in 1828. An agreed amount was later paid to his widow, final settlement of his outstanding bills and those of others being made in 1832. The total amount spent on improvements had now reached the staggering sum of £113,355.[5]

When the Reform Act of 1832 swept away most of the inequalities in parliamentary representation there were moves for a similar reform of local government. A Municipal Corporations Commission was set up, and two of its commissioners took evidence at Exeter in November 1833. They noted its system of local government, which was exercised by a mayor elected annually by the freemen and the city chamber. The latter consisted of eight aldermen, elected for life by the freemen, and 15 common councillors elected for life by the city chamber itself. The commissioners were critical of the over-expenditure on the canal, though there was the excellent defence that expert advice had been sought from Thomas Telford. Even so, under cross-examination Alderman Sanders said of the canal:

> . . . if the Chamber had forseen the heavy expenditure which it would have led to, they would not have subscribed to it, even for the sake of the citizens of Exeter.[6]

The city chamber was reformed by the Municipal Corporations Act of 1835 and the new council appointed a committee to examine the expenditure on the canal. The findings disclosed an astonishing state of ineptitude. No contracts had been made in writing for any part of the work, nor had many of the improvements ever received the sanction of the city chamber. Payments of nearly £90,000 had been made by the treasurer to James Green without any authority for the one party to pay and the other to draw these amounts. The principal sums paid by Mr. Crockett, treasurer, until the passing of the 1829 Exeter Canal Act, were:

Timber	£6,330
Millwright	£5,545
Culm and coals	£1,834
Lime and other stone ..	£5,937
Iron	£2,199
Cartage	£788
Purchase of land	£997
Freight	£1,574
Labour	£48,738
Law charges	£1,611
Engineer	£3,954
Sundries	£4,865
Beer	£1,497
Mason	£10,611
Incidentals	£520

The committee noted that Mr. Crockett was a partner in the city brewery which had provided the beer and that he had paid interest on the outstanding account without any authority from the city chamber. They decided that they could not sanction the expenditure on the canal improvements 'a measure which their predecessors (who had the greatest interest in so doing) took care to avoid'. Instead, they recommended that some competent judges be appointed to compare the actual value of the work and material supplied with the outlay, to 'determine what ulterior measure' should be taken by the council. They concluded that the scheme for the extension and improvements:

EXETER CANAL.

ACCOUNT OF EXTRA WORKS AND SUMS EXPENDED WHICH WERE NOT INCLUDED IN ESTIMATES.

	£.	s.	d.
Interest and commission at Bank	1,788	2	5
Act of Parliament	802	10	5
House at Turf, forming ground, piles, &c. . . .	800	0	0
It having been found by experience, that the set of the tide below Turf lock was such as greatly to obstruct the entrance of vessels, it became necessary to make an embankment on the mud on the east side of the entrance channel, which completely remedied the evil . .	1,000	0	0
Repairs to Topsham Quay, dredging, &c. . . .	800	0	0
Topsham lock, &c. occasioned by inhabitants of Topsham . .	3,500	0	0
Repairs to banks through Sir John Duckworth's marshes, occasioned by breaking in of floods	150	0	0
Countess Weir Bridge, toll-house, and masonry . . .	1,200	0	0
Widening, deepening, and straightening Alphington Brook, from Countess Weir Bridge to above double lock; repairing gates at the sluice, &c. as required by Mr. Cartwright on behalf of Sir L. Palk . .	600	0	0
Alphington Brook, at present entrance into the river, and extras occasioned by Mr. Davey's opposition	500	0	0
Dredging river Exe from Exe Bridge, and deepening the river at the Quay and to King's Arms Sluice	600	0	0
Repairing and stoning banks of river from Exe Bridge to King's Arms Sluice several times	200	0	0
Boundary walls, gates, &c. surrounding the basin . . .	900	0	0
House at New Cut Close, with repairs and alterations . .	200	0	0
Roads to and about the basin	130	0	0
Planting banks with witheys, dags, sedges, &c. . . .	300	0	0
Mooring posts, additional fences, gates, &c. . . .	200	0	0
Repair of weirs, hatches, &c.	300	0	0
Cowley Bridge repairs and alterations	150	0	0
Northernhay improvements, under direction of committee . .	180	0	0
Steam-engine-dredger and barges, and other materials on hand .	900	0	0
Colleton Crescent excavation, wall above, alteration of Mr. Kennaway's cellars, paving and making roads to and on the quay, &c. .	3,000	0	0
Repairs on old canal from June, 1826, to December, 1828, two years and a half, and making alterations and general repairs of buildings at double lock	2,000	0	0
Expences of Telford and Holden	178	3	6
	£20,378	16	4

Figure 11. James Green's additional expenses for the extension to Turf.

. . . was commenced without due deliberation, prosecuted in unbounded extravagance, and has terminated in the dissipation of the enormous sum of £113,000 of public property, producing no return.[7]

The report of the committee was made to the city council on 4 October 1836 and subsequently published. The council accused James Green of neglect and, after several letters had been exchanged, he produced an account of the additional expenses not included in any of his estimates (*see* opposite). Reporting on many difficulties encountered in making the improvements, he ended:

> With all these circumstances the Navigation Committee were, from time to time, made fully acquainted, and the works as they proceeded had their entire sanction; and the attention I constantly paid to the execution of the works enables me to state my conviction, that if it were possible to divest the accounts of the sums expended in the unforeseen and unavoidable difficulties, they would be found to amount to at least £25,000 over and above the items hereinbefore particularized; and I feel very confident that, on a full explanation of all the circumstances to any practical and competent judge of such works, he would be of the same opinion.[8]

The council had invited members of the former city chamber to meet them in August to discuss James Green's report. At the conclusion of that meeting they adopted a face-saving formula, resolving:

> . . . the benefits which will arise to the Public from the improved Navigation of the Port will steadily progress as they have to this time and justify an Expenditure which, although it has very considerably exceeded the intentions of those who embarked in it, was commenced and concluded with a view to public advantage alone, and without any private affection or partial respect.[9]

The city chamber had tried to come to terms with the challenge of railways and, when approached by the promoters of the Bristol & Exeter Railway, they promised their support. The Bill for that railway, published in 1836, proposed that the Exeter terminal should be on the south-west side of the canal basin. The new city council were not sure what action to take, for at first they opposed the Bill, then consented to it, and finally petitioned against it to parliament, as they wished to retain full control of the basin. Parliament recognised this fact by upholding their rights when the Act was passed the same year but the terminal remained unaltered. However, the opposition to the Act must have been sufficient for the Bristol & Exeter Railway to look elsewhere, eventually siting their terminus at St David's, a mile to the north-west of the canal basin.

In July 1837 the navigation committee were informed that the canal dues for the quarter ending at midsummer amounted to £2,596, the highest for any quarter. Some of this money, of course, was used to pay the salaries of the canal staff. Thomas Perryman, lock-keeper at Double locks, received £33 12s. 6d., plus a house, field and garden, though he had to pay an assistant from that salary.

Similarly, Nicholas Lewis of Turf lock was paid £43 8s. 0d. and had a house and garden, also having to pay for an assistant from this amount. The job of lock-keeper carried with it the trade of innkeeper, as both houses were licensed and had stabling and accommodation. This was to be the downfall of Lewis, who lost his job at Turf in February 1841 through being 'incapacitated from performing the duties of his Office' owing to drink. Perryman died the following April and was succeeded by his son. The canal labourers were, at this time, being paid a wage of 14s. 0d. a week.[10]

There were eight labourers on the regular establishment in September 1841 and two carpenters making a barge. The towage establishment no longer existed, having been let out to contract in August 1838 (*see* opposite). On the canal, several parts of the eastern bank between Topsham bridge and Turf required immediate repair and the entrance to Turf lock needed dredging. The western bank was said to 'require anxious care' and the balance beams of the lower gates at Topsham lock were almost broken into two. The navigation committee agreed that all these works should be put in hand.[11]

Some of the damage to the banks could have been caused by the steamer *Alert,* given permission in September 1840 to pass through the locks on Sundays 'until the pleasure of the Council be known'. The experiment could not have been a success, because the steamer was put up for sale soon afterwards. A year later the Canal Surveyor, George Julian, reported that the dredger was almost worn out and the accompanying barge badly decayed. Nothing was done, and in September 1842 he had to remove the dredger from the canal to prevent it sinking. The city council then decided to sell it by auction but failed to realise that a replacement dredger would be needed. The realisation came quickly, Julian informing the navigation committee in December that one ship could get no further than 500 yards from Turf lock owing to the lack of dredging. This and many other craft had to discharge their cargoes at other ports. It was then agreed that the dredger be repaired if possible and that a dredger barge be hired from the River Commissioners. Two months later *The Peamore,* under the command of Captain Anning, ran into the barge and caused considerable|damage.[12]

The River Commissioners had been appointed by the powers of the Exeter Port and Dues Act of 19 June 1840. One of their purposes was to preserve and provide safe navigational conditions on the River Exe and its estuary. To achieve this, four commissioners were appointed by the Topsham electors and three by Exeter City Council, and a salaried clerk looked after the administration. The responsibilities of the commissioners included dredging, buoyage and pilotage.[13]

Having decided to farm out the canal tolls, the navigation committee put them up for auction with the town dues on 2 March 1843. They were let for a term of three years, from the day after Lady Day, at an annual rental of £9,905 to Jonas Levy. The great prosperity of the canal at this time is exemplified by a description of the canal basin, written before the railways came to Exeter:

I have seen from 20 to 30 vessels, two or three deep, lying there, and the ground covered with various goods and packages ... the import of

THE COUNCIL

OF

EXETER

Are desirous to receive TENDERS

from Persons willing to PROVIDE HORSES and MEN for
TOWING the VESSELS on the EXETER CANAL for
THREE YEARS, from Michaelmas next, subject to such
Regulations as shall be laid down by the Council, to ensure
the regular and effective performance of the work.

The Council are also desirous of receiving TENDERS
for REPAIRING the Towing Paths and the Surface and
Interior Slopes of the Canal Banks, to the Water's Edge,
and the whole of the Exterior Banks as far as regards ordinary and usual wear and tear, and to Cleanse and keep in
Repair the Ditches, for the like period of THREE YEARS.

Any person may Tender for both works, or for either
separately; but in case of a joint Tender, the sum for which
each branch of the work will be performed, must be specified.

The Tenders are requested to be sent to the TOWN
CLERK'S OFFICE, on or before the 20th day of August instant.

By Order,

JOHN GIDLEY, Town Clerk.

8th August, 1838.

Figure 12.   Notice seeking tenders for horse towing and repairs.

coals was immense, the surrounding towns and villages being supplied
by the merchants. There were two trading companies for merchandise
having about six vessels each, the tonnage from 120 to 128, sailing to
and from London weekly, weather permitting.[14]

Already the railways were approaching, and the Bristol & Exeter reached
Taunton in 1842. Other routes were planned and, at the city council's request,
a sub-committee was formed in September 1843 'to watch the proceedings
relative to an intended railway from this City to Plymouth and to report to the
Council as they may think proper'. The railway age reached Exeter on 1 May
1844 when a special train of the Bristol & Exeter Railway, appropriately hauled
by the locomotive *City of Exeter,* steamed into St David's station. The trade
of the canal was almost immediately affected and the mortgagees of the canal
property became worried that the interest due to them might not be met.[15]

Maurice Ceeley Trevillian, one of the mortgagees, instituted a suit in the
Court of Chancery on 22 April 1845 on behalf of himself and the other creditors
of the canal. They wanted Exeter Corporation to repay all the money borrowed
under the powers of the 1829 Exeter Canal Act, claiming that some of this had
been misapplied in the repayment of loans made before the passing of the Act.
Interim relief, by the appointment of a receiver to administer two-thirds of the
income derived from the lease of tolls, was granted. It was considered that the
other one-third of the lease related to town dues which were not connected
with the canal.[16]

The city council was anxious to attract more trade to the canal and sought the
opinion of merchants, traders and their own clerks. One of these, Mr. Stabback,
pointed out that high charges were causing a loss of trade. The average toll was
2s. 6d. per ton, with a similar sum for cartage from the quay to the consignee's
address in Exeter. Goods landed at Topsham did not attract any charges, other
than 4d. per ton if landed at the town quay, and the rate for road transport
from Topsham to the consignee at Exeter was 3s. 6d. per ton. This showed an
average saving of at least 1s. 6d. per ton, and more if the cost of towage on
the canal was taken into account. Stabback also mentioned the effect of the
Bristol & Exeter Railway upon the canal trade:

> The whole of the Trade from Bristol and Wales has totally ceased and
> that from Liverpool and Gloucester generally lessened and we must
> naturally look forward to further loss in the Plymouth and Cornish
> trade when the South Devon line is in operation.[17]

Stabback and all others consulted recommended that the canal tolls and
dues be cut. This recommendation was accepted in March 1846, changes being
made as follows:

Cargo Dues
    Coal from 1s. 8d. to 1s. 0d. per ton.
    General goods (other than wine and spirits) cut by one-third. [Wine
    and spirits charges remained unchanged].

Passage tolls per ton
  Vessels of 110 tons and over from 9d. to 4d.
  Vessels between 11 and 109 tons from 6d. to 4d.
  Vessels of 10 tons and under, flat charge of 5s. 0d. reduced to 4s. 0d.

Towage charges each way
  Vessels of 60 tons and over, 1s. 4d. per registered ton.
  Vessels between 40 and 60 tons, flat charge of 6s. 0d.
  Vessels between 30 and 39 tons, flat charge of 5s. 0d.
  Vessels under 30 tons register, flat charge of 4s. 0d.

Not surprisingly, as a result of railway competition, Jonas Levy did not want to continue his lease of the canal tolls and town dues after Lady Day 1846. Richard Banfill was then appointed chief clerk at the wharfinger's office and Messrs. Stabback and Tothill given the jobs of second and third clerks under him. These arrangements, as those of the reduction in dues, tolls and towage, now had to be agreed with a committee of the canal creditors, a situation that was to hamper the administration for many years to come.[18]

Exeter corporation had depended on the profits from the canal to help to run the city and, with the income now appropriated by the receiver, they had to look for new sources of income. A borough rate was levied in April 1846, one newspaper commenting at the time 'the vigilance of the citizens would ensure that it did not become permanent'. The city council, too, hoped that it would be only a temporary measure, as indicated by a report of the special finance committee in December 1846:

> They also express their hope that the pending arrangement with the Canal creditors may soon be brought to a termination, and that the result may have the effect of restoring to the Council some portion of the Canal income; they beg to add their recommendation that every means in the power of the Council be adopted to prevent the further progress of litigation.

The city council was partially successful in its objective, for the case of the canal creditors was eventually heard in the Easter law term 1853. The borough rate is a different story![19]

From 1846 onwards there was a steady growth in railway competition. Proposals had been made for a line from Exeter to Exmouth via Powderham and Starcross in 1825, though nothing happened at that time. Starcross was linked by rail to Exeter in May 1846 by the opening of the South Devon Railway. The route was extended to Newton Abbot that same year and reached Plymouth in 1849. In 1851 railway sidings were laid at Teignmouth quay, giving direct access to and from the main line, and enabling the port to compete with the Exeter Canal coal trade. The long-planned railway from Exeter to Crediton was also opened in 1851 and extended to Barnstaple in 1854 and Okehampton in 1871.

Plans for the Exeter to Exmouth route were revived in 1846 when two rival companies introduced Bills into parliament. The Exeter, Topsham & Exmouth

Railway Bill was opposed by the city council, because it would interfere with
their interests in the canal and Topsham quay. From a junction with the South
Devon Railway, it was planned to cross the canal and River Exe, then go by way
of Topsham and Lympstone to Exmouth. The station at Topsham was to be
within 350 yards of the quay. Opposition to this scheme was successful and
the Bill thrown out of parliament. The rival Exeter & Exmouth Railway,
planned to run entirely on the west side of the River Exe, received the support
of the city council and obtained its Act. The powers were not implemented and
Exmouth had to wait until 1861 for a railway.[20]

The canal surveyor, George Julian, was acutely aware of the problems of
transport between the basin and the railways and suggested that the canal
should have a link with the Bristol & Exeter. His suggestion was, apparently,
ignored. Three years later, in 1849, he tried again by proposing two alternative
schemes. One was for a connection with the South Devon Railway by a 100-ft.-
long tramway from the basin. The other envisaged using 5-ton flat-bottomed
barges, fitted with wheels, which could be floated on the River Exe from the
quay to St David's station, by-passing Head weir by means of an inclined plane
similar to those then in use on the Bude Canal. Again, nothing happened.[21]

Earlier, in June 1847, another attempt had been made to let the canal tolls
but nobody was interested. The next year there were complaints about the poor
towage facilities, many craft having to wait at Turf because horses were not
available or else too weak for work. William Langmead, the towage contractor,
was admonished by the navigation committee. This had no effect as the complaints continued. Possibly as a result of these difficulties the steamer *Malcolm
Brown* was allowed to travel under her own steam along the canal at a speed
not to exceed 3 m.p.h. It was a new trading venture for passengers and goods
between Exeter and London but did not last for long as the captain blatantly
ignored the speed limit, even when the canal surveyor was aboard. Steamships
were once again prohibited on the canal. A larger ship, the biggest to use the
canal at that time, was a 330-ton barque with a length of 100 feet and beam of
25ft. 6in. which was refitting at the basin in January 1848.[22]

Costs were now being keenly watched and at the end of 1848 Julian was asked
to prepare a written report on the labour used, to see if any savings could be
made. Economies were certainly necessary, with competition now coming from
steamships as well as from the railways. The navigation committee were told
in August 1850 that the canal had lost nearly all of its London trade when a
steamship service began between London and Plymouth, carrying goods at
3s. 6d. per ton. The income fell to £4,610 in this year.[23]

Julian decided to enter the Exeter coal trade himself. The city coal merchants
protested, being particularly annoyed that his ship *Alpha* had got stuck on the
sill of King's Arms sluice and blocked the entrance to the quay for a whole
day. They complained that he was quick to report any damage that they might
have caused, yet failed to notify any done by his own craft. Julian told the
navigation committee that it was the first he had heard of the mishap and then
explained why he had entered the coal trade:

. . . there is a general dissatisfaction at the manner in which the inhabitants of Exeter have been served with Coals, by fact of the inferior Articles having been imposed at high prices . . . the interests of the canal have suffered and would be completely destroyed if measures had not been taken to preserve them.[24]

Julian's business was the subject of further discussion in July 1851 after another petition by the coal merchants. He was given the choice of ceasing to trade or else to resign from his position as canal surveyor. He chose the latter, George W. Cumming being appointed to succeed him in March 1852. There was a change of towage contractor the following year, the choice of George Newton ending the many complaints about a lack of horses. Cumming also solved the problems of having to hire a dredger barge, gaining authorisation for a new one to be built with the appropriate machinery, the cost not to exceed £160.[25]

The cause of the canal creditors finally came up for hearing in the Court of Chancery on 25 April 1853 before Vice-Chancellor Kindersley. He decided that the corporation had not committed any breach of trust in applying money raised under the powers of the 1829 Act to repay earlier loans for the construction of the canal. The receivership of the canal income was continued, all accounts not required for maintenance or the payment of interest to the canal creditors having been paid into Court since 1845. The costs of this action were to be paid from the funds already held.

The canal creditors decided to appeal against this judgement with the object of gaining a lien on other parts of the corporation's property, sufficient to secure their interest payments. The corporation, on the other hand, tried to prevent further litigation and took steps to consolidate their corporate debt. This action was encouraged by the then buoyant state of the money market, but before a Bill could be introduced into parliament the market became depressed and put an end to this proposal.

The Appeal by the canal creditors was heard by Lord Justices Knight-Bruce and Turner, who reversed the judgement of Vice-Chancellor Kindersley by deciding that the corporation had not been authorised by the 1829 Exeter Canal Act to repay earlier borrowings. The prior mortgages, which had amounted to £34,500, constituted a debt to the canal creditors. They therefore had a lien on the corporation's estates, other than those of the canal, comprising the property already mortgaged and which still remained vested in their possession. Final judgement was reserved, to give time for an agreement to be made between the plaintiffs and defendants.

Agreement was reached between the two parties and embodied in a Deed of Arrangement on 20 June 1857. The terms, in brief, were:

1. No claim to be made for arrears of interest prior to Christmas 1854, After payment of Court costs, the nett receipts held by the Court would be used towards interest outstanding in 1854.
2. From Christmas 1854 interest was to be reduced to 4½ per cent. per annum, to be paid from the nett canal income and any surplus income

of the city council after the usual corporate expenses had been met. The interest account would be over a three-year period, at the end of which any arrears would be given up or any surplus applied in the reduction of the canal debt. The city council were authorised to purchase canal mortgages at the current market price from any such surplus, so that they could be cancelled.

3. Corporation property valued at £34,536 was to be mortgaged to the trustees of the canal creditors without interest. This property was to be sold as the opportunity arose, and the proceeds used to purchase canal mortgages for cancellation.

4. The city council would continue to manage the corporate property 'according to the spirit of this agreement'.

5. The chancery receivership would cease from 24 June 1855, a nominee of the canal creditors being appointed in his place. He would have all the powers of a chancery receiver and 'no outlay exceeding the Sum of £200 in any one year, except for ordinary Repairs, Labour, Salaries, and Rates and Taxes, shall be made without the consent of the person so appointed'.

It has often been said that the only person who gains from litigation is a lawyer, which seems to have been true so far as the chancery receivership was concerned. Of the £2,964 that had been paid into the Court until 1854, all but £27 was swallowed up by legal fees.[26]

In spite of the economies that were being made there were the occasional acts of generosity. One was for James Gill who, at the age of 86, was now 'past labour' on the canal. The navigation committee granted him a pension of 15s. 0d. per week for life from January 1854 though unfortunately he did not live for very long afterwards. The committee also met to consider ways of escape for persons who might accidentally fall into the basin. At times they were not so quick to act. Robert Tothill, third clerk at the quay, wrote to the surveyor on 4 November 1856 to ask that his cottage at the basin be made wind- and water-tight before winter set in. George Cumming, the surveyor, brought this to the attention of the committee at their meeting the same day and was asked to arrange for specifications and estimates to be ready for the following meeting. This took place on 1 January, the estimate being between £12 and £14, and the committee decided to seek tenders. On 5 February a tender for £10 10s. 0d. was accepted, but there was a further delay whilst a contract was drawn up for repairs. One can only hope that the winter of 1856–57 was a mild and dry one for the sake of the Tothill family.[27]

The delays in the Tothill case were, perhaps, a foretaste of things to come for the navigation committee themselves. The canal creditors were to exercise a stranglehold over finances which, in course of time, would affect general repairs and dredging.

Chapter Six

FIGHTING FOR FINANCE (1858–1883)

WHILST THE CORPORATION and the canal creditors were engaged with the Deed of Arrangement after the Chancery suit, there were other problems for the navigation committee to consider. In 1853 proposals for an Exeter & Exmouth Railway were revived and included two routes that would affect the canal. One was for a line from Exeter quay to Exmouth, the other for a branch from the South Devon Railway to cross over the canal and River Exe near Topsham and then follow the eastern side of the estuary to Exmouth. The city council were urged by both the navigation committee and the canal creditors to negotiate with the railway, so that it could make a connection with the canal basin. For reasons best known to themselves the city council decided to oppose the plans but an Act of 1855 authorised both routes, though provision had to be made for a branch line to the canal basin.

Plans for the Exeter & Exmouth Railway came unstuck when the shareholders of the South Devon and Bristol & Exeter railways objected to the proposed lease of the new line. Eventually an agreement was made between the Exeter & Exmouth and London & South Western railways. The latter had plans to build a branch line from Exeter to Topsham where, it was agreed, it would link with the southern half of the proposed Exeter & Exmouth Railway. The remainder of the authorised route from Topsham across the Exe estuary and canal to the South Devon Railway was abandoned by an Act of 1858, the new joint line opening on 1 May 1861. The previous year the London & South Western Railway had reached Exeter from Salisbury, providing a second line to London. A new terminus was built at Queen Street (now Exeter Central) for the opening, and a link line between St David's and Queen Street completed in 1862.

Though the Exeter Canal still remained without its railway link, Topsham was more fortunate. The London & South Western Railway bought Topsham quay and extended it 80 feet outwards into the estuary. Three small quays between it and the steamer quay were filled in so that the whole area made a large wharf. It was connected by a short siding with the Exeter & Exmouth Railway at Topsham. The coming of the railway helped to arrest the declining trade of the port and one family was quick to seize upon the opportunity for expansion. It was to be short-lived, as Exeter dock opened in 1868 with better access and facilities.

The Holmans had been associated with Topsham from the 16th century and about 1846 John Holman bought a shipyard from the Davy family. (It was

Robert Davy who had taken the city chamber to Court in 1827, resulting in the construction of Topsham lock opposite the town.) John Holman, besides being a ship-builder, was also a master mariner and had founded the Mutual Marine Insurance Association. Between 1857 and 1866 seven ships were launched from his yards, including two barques of over 500 tons each. In 1858 the Holman family had a fleet of 12 sailing ships trading to the Mediterranean, West Indies and South America, several having been built at Topsham. Some of the craft were sheathed in copper, yellow metal or zinc and later an iron-clad ship was built. Already the era of the sailing ship was drawing to a close, and in 1870 the Holmans bought their first steam-powered auxiliary, the *City of Exeter*. Gradually the rest of the fleet was replaced, first by steam-powered auxiliaries and later by fully steam-powered craft. Then, at the turn of the century, the entire fleet was sold, all shipbuilding ceased and the great days of the port of Topsham were over. In more recent years one of John Holman's descendants, Miss D. Holman, opened a small maritime museum in a sail loft at 25 The Strand, Topsham. This houses many relics of the Holman family and their fleet and, appropriately, is in premises that were once part of the ship-building business.[1]

The growth of the railway system caused the loss of most of the coastwise trade of the Exeter Canal and imports of coal further declined in the face of this competition. The principal imports in the 1860s were wines, hides, and timber, coal having lost its position as the premier cargo. A history of Exeter, published in 1861, gave some reason for the fall of trade in its description of the canal:

> Unfortunately this great work was undertaken just before steam navigation at sea was adopted. The proportions of Turf lock are there-fore not such as would be now observed . . . The Chamber, moreover, had always regarded their canal, not as a mere water-communication for the use of Exeter, but as a great trunk route whence branches were to be carried into the remoter inland districts, so as to connect them with the English Channel . . . they rendered whatever assistance they could to a railway from Crediton to their canal, when railways else-where were dreaded or ridiculed. How they were defeated few remem-ber . . . To connect the railway system with the canal is now a very difficult task, and it is not easy to foretell when these great engineering works, which were planned for beneficial co-operation, shall cease to be antagonistic.[2]

The city council and canal creditors agreed on the necessity of railway com-munication with the canal, a joint meeting of the two bodies in 1861 suggesting that a horse tramway be laid. They had two alternatives in mind, either a link between the basin and the South Devon Railway, or between the quay and the Bristol & Exeter Railway at St David's station. There were negotiations with the South Devon Railway and the projected Teign Valley Railway from Exeter to Heathfield in 1864 and in the following year an arrangement was made with the South Devon for broad and standard gauge lines between the canal basin and St David's station.

The two different gauges were necessary as the South Devon and Bristol & Exeter had adopted Brunel's 7-ft. broad gauge, whilst the London & South Western and the Crediton railways were laid to Stephenson's 4ft. 8½in. gauge. The broad gauge route was opened on 10 June 1867, its principal use being the carriage of timber. The standard gauge line took longer and, though laid by 1870, formal agreement for its use was not sanctioned for many years. It was not until October 1876 that the wharfinger was able to tell the navigation committee that 'a truck load of timber was brought into the basin a few days since by the narrow gauge line'. The line was made by laying a third rail within the broad gauge track and this dual gauge continued until 1892, when the Great Western Railway abandoned the broad gauge.[3]

About 1861, long before a railway link was made with the canal basin, a new level road was made from the Exe bridge to St David's station. Despite the fact that it made an easier route between the two places, it failed to satisfy the Exeter traders who still complained at the expense of double transhipment from ship to cart and cart to railway wagon. The transport charges from the basin were not the only source of grievance, for there were also constant complaints about the canal tolls. Eventually the city council formed a 'Special Committee on Canal Dues' and a conference with the shipowners using the canal was held on 2 February 1866. Their chief complaints were about the high costs incurred in using the waterway, similar grievances about pilotage from the mouth of the Exe estuary, the inconvenience of King's Arms sluice and the charges for ballasting.[4]

Looking at these points in more detail, it is difficult to see what action the city council could have taken to appease the complainants, as the canal was effectively controlled by the canal creditors. No reduction of tolls could be made without their prior consent and they were reluctant to give this unless assured of a definite increase in trade. Pilotage charges were a necessary expense owing to the gradual silting of the Exe estuary. Some people considered that this silting was a direct result of the storms of 1824 which had breached the natural sea wall at Dawlish Warren, washing sand into the bed of the estuary. The complaints about King's Arm sluice were justified, as it was kept closed in times of flood. Here also there was little that could be done to ease the delay for craft waiting to berth at the quay. If the gates were to remain open in flood-times, a great amount of silt would be carried down the canal with obvious disadvantages. The final complaint about ballasting was basically caused by the lack of return cargoes for most craft. Their owners resented the charge of 3d. per ton for ballast in addition to the charge for loading.

The special committee examined these complaints in detail and reported in 1868 that the high level of tolls and dues was an important factor in the decline of trade. A suggested reduction for goods brought up the canal by the London traders was sanctioned by the canal creditors, but otherwise the grievances went unanswered. One minor concession for the improvement of trade was made in

1868 when the navigation committee agreed to allow steamers to use the canal, providing they kept to a 3 m.p.h. speed limit and that the ship's screw was a full 6 feet above the bottom of the cut.[5]

Amidst the unending worries about finance there was the occasional celebration, as in 1863 when the chief clerk, Richard Banfill, was authorised to spend up to £1 10s. 0d. 'to procure a star to be illuminated with gas on the night of 10 March in honour of the marriage of the Prince of Wales'. Economies with dredging were made in 1867; Bodley Brothers of Exeter were engaged to carry out the job at a contract price of 9d. per ton, the navigation committee supplying the dredger and associated equipment.[6]

Soon afterwards the state of King's Arms sluice, Double locks and Turf lock gave cause for concern. The extensive repairs needed could not be undertaken without the consent of the canal creditors, so a visit to the sites was made by their representatives. Afterwards they agreed 'that the same should be commenced with as little delay as circumstances will admit of'. A few days later William Beardmore, a civil engineer from London, was engaged at £5 5s. 0d. per day plus expenses to inspect and report upon the canal.[7]

His instructions were:

1. To report on the state of the Canal, and what is required for putting the same in good repair, and a safe working condition, also as to an effectual and economical method of carrying out the works, and estimate of probable expense.
2. Report on whether means can be adopted for supplying the Canal with water in order to keep up Traffic with the Basin during the works at King's Arms sluice.
3. Advise whether any means can be adopted to relieve the Canal from pressure in case of Floods.
4. Report on what additional work should be necessary to admit larger vessels than can now enter Turf, say about 30 feet additional length, with an Estimate of the Cost.

William Beardmore's preliminary report found that:

> . . . The General appearance of the Canal is substantial and safe in respect of the banks and walls of Locks and Bridges, and the depth appeared to be well maintained considering little dredging has been done or other expense incurred.

A more detailed report with costings appeared in September 1867. Dealing first with King's Arms sluice, he noted that new gates and masonry repairs were required. A dam would have to be built across the canal on the River Exe side of the flood-gates and stop-planks fitted into the grooves below the gates, so that the water could be pumped out and repairs begin. If possible, these works should take place at the same time as those proposed for Double locks. Otherwise, the water supply to the canal would have to be maintained by a pipe or trunk passing over the ground at the back of the gate-keeper's house, a sluice of about

2ft. square controlling the flow. The time taken to complete these repairs he thought 'cannot be less than four weeks' and the cost £1,200, though £300 could be saved if the temporary water supply was not needed.[8]

Double locks also needed new gates, which, it was suggested, should be made beforehand instead of the customary practice of building up large gates piecemeal in the lock. Beardmore suggested that the old pair of upper gates could be broken up and the timber used to build the new pair for the lower gates. He also proposed the use of lifting tackle to fit them as, in any event, this would be needed for Turf lock. Apart from the new gates, repairs were also necessary for the lock sills and to the hollow quoins (in which the heel posts of the lock gates turned). A dam would have to be built across the tail of Double locks and the water level in the lower pound from Turf reduced to 5 feet to ease the pressure. The upper pound to the basin and King's Arm sluice would also have to be drained and that is why he recommended that the two repair jobs be carried out at the same time. The length of the stoppage was reckoned to be 'about six weeks' and the cost £2,300.

Turf lock presented the biggest problem of all. Water was escaping through a swallow hole on the canal bottom, above the upper gates, and flowing under the lock to 'blow up' through the apron below the lower gates. Beardmore was worried about the state of the foundations and recommended that every effort be made to examine and repair the lock and its gates whilst it was still in water. Heavy tackle and lifting gear would be needed for the gates and, possibly, a diver if any unforeseen difficulties arose. He suggested that more stone and Portland cement be dropped into the swallow hole to reduce the escape of water, noting that a similar action by the canal surveyor, George Cumming, about ten years ago had prevented a disaster. He also proposed planking over the lower lock apron to strengthen it and to resist water rising through it, estimating that the total cost of the job would be £1,450. A warning was given that the repairs would not leave the lock in an entirely satisfactory state because there were some inherent defects in its construction, and so caution would always be needed in its use and subsequent repair.

Beardmore considered that Turf lock ought to be dealt with in summer 1868 though Double locks and King's Arms sluice could be deferred for a further year. At present some urgent repairs were being carried out on the canal, as suggested in his preliminary report, and when these were completed he would be able to make a better judgement of the situation. In addition to the cost of repairs to Turf lock, Double locks and King's Arms sluice, he allowed for contingencies of £1,050, making an overall total of £6,000.

Referring to the question of flood relief, he did not think that the canal would be in danger in times of ordinary flood, but proposed that dredged spoil be used to raise the level of the marshes between King's Arms sluice and Trew's weir. There was no advantage to be gained by opening the gates at King's Arms sluice, as the flood waters would carry silt into the canal.

The final portion of the report was concerned with the proposal to lengthen Turf lock by 30 feet. The most practical way of achieving this was to extend it beyond the present upper gates. Beardmore considered that the expense would be very great in proportion to the advantage to be gained, especially as a stoppage of more than three months would be needed for the improvement. The cost was expected to be at least £7,700, but £1,800 could be saved on the other repairs scheduled for Turf lock. For example, the lengthening of the lock chamber would eliminate the problem of water escaping down the swallow hole.

Alternative plans were produced for a complete reconstruction of the canal, and Beardmore wrote:

> . . . we know that the smaller class of Vessels fit to go through your present Canal are yearly becoming more scarce, and there is a great probability that in a few years time all important foreign Trade will be carried on in Vessels that could not pass through your Canal. With these views and considering how great a detriment to the Trade is a long stoppage of the Canal, I think that the construction of new and larger Locks at Turf and near the site of Double Lock, independent of the present navigation, would be the best way of proceeding if your Funds are equal and the future prospects should be deemed worth the Expenditure.

His plans were for locks 220ft. long and 34ft. wide, the canal being widened to allow the through passage of craft able to pass the locks. The estimated cost was:

New lock at Turf	£26,000
New Double lock, with a ½ mile of new cut..	£25,000
Widening entrance to Exeter basin and King's Arms sluice ..	£7,500
Cutting away bends, widening bridges, etc.	£4,500
Dredging throughout to a depty of 14ft.	£5,000
Allowance for contingencies	£7,000
	£75,000

Beardmore's report has been set out in some detail to show that railway competition was not the only reason for a decline in trade. The limited dimensions of the locks were a major cause for its diversion to other places, a situation that was to be aggravated by the opening of Exmouth Dock in 1868 with its direct rail access to Exeter. The tight control of finances by the canal creditors had already resulted in a low standard of maintenance and dredging, as noted in Beardmore's report. His hopes of a complete reconstruction to permit larger craft to use the canal were doomed from the outset, as neither the city council nor the canal creditors were willing to provide the money. Indeed, the latter voted it to be 'totally unnecessary'.[9]

Under the terms of settlement of the dispute between the corporation and the canal creditors, set out in the Deed of Arrangement of 1857, the city council had redeemed the statutory mortgages of £34,500 at a cost of less than half that amount. The Deed of Arrangement also provided for any surplus income of the corporation to be paid over to the receiver for the canal creditors, to help to guarantee the 4½ per cent. per annum interest due on the mortgages. However, after the redemption of the statutory mortgages, the corporation arranged their affairs from 1866 onwards so that no surplus income arose.[10]

Work began on the repairs to Turf lock in June 1868, the canal being closed to all traffic other than barges (which could enter through Topsham lock) from 10 July. Soon afterwards it was found that more extensive repairs were needed, the canal surveyor reporting that the lock apron above the inner gates needed entire renewal at an estimated expense of £450. Beardmore was called in to make an examination and found that water was percolating freely through the apron and wing walls of the lock. This indicated that both the apron and foundations were hollow or otherwise defective. He recommended shoring up the lock, writing 'I consider the case altogether one of great difficulty, and some danger'. The work proved to be more awkward than had been estimated, the overall cost of the repairs to the lock amounting to £4,738, and the canal did not re-open to traffic until 25 February 1869.[11]

The rearrangement of the corporation's finances to avoid payment of any surplus income to the canal creditors, coupled with the expensive repairs to Turf lock, meant that there was virtually no money available to pay the interest due on the canal mortgages. A deputation from the canal creditors saw the navigation committee in May 1870 'to press upon the Committee the desirability of watching the expenditure upon the Canal with a view to keeping it as low as possible'. Amongst the economies suggested were the letting out of the maintenance to contract and the cessation of dredging. The latter was a strange suggestion to make as the silting of the Exe estuary had narrowed the channel between Star-cross sands and Lympstone sands to about 60yds. width. The corporation, fearing that access to the canal could be blocked, had begun to dredge the lower estuary in 1870 and thereafter kept a watch to prevent further silting or shoaling which might obstruct the navigable channel.[12]

In 1871 the total of the dues collected was £3,206, and in 1874 they had dropped to £1,993, a decrease of some 40 per cent. within three years. One change made in this period was the takeover of the towage when the existing lease ran out in 1873. The same year the long-awaited repairs were made to King's Arms sluice at an expense of about £800.[13]

Apart from the corporation and the canal creditors, other people had an interest in the future of the canal, including Captain Charles Halford Thompson, R.A. In August 1876 he published *A Letter to the Bondholders of the Canal*, setting out his views on the ways to improve trade to the port of Exeter. Several of his suggestions were similar to the points raised by the shipowners when they met the city council special committee in February 1866. They included:

1. An alteration to the inefficiently performed system of pilotage and a considerable reduction in the charges for it. The current charge of £6 7s. 0d. for a foreign ship of 200 tons was exhorbitantly high compared with the £2 12s. 3d. charged for a similar vessel at Newcastle, Hartlepool, Sunderland, or Middlesborough.

2. The abolition of town dues. These made an additional tax on goods entering the city via the canal, whilst those coming by rail escaped this tax.
3. The use of steam power on the canal, both by keeping a steam tug stationed at Turf and by allowing steam-ships to travel along the canal under their own power.
4. No charge to be made for ballast taken from Exeter quay.
5. Increased facilities for the dispatch of goods by rail from the canal basin at Exeter. The standard gauge line had been completed for some time, but formal agreement for its use was still awaited from the South Devon Railway.[14]

Captain Thompson continued his campaign to increase trade on the canal by reading a paper on the subject to the Exeter Chamber of Commerce on 21 September 1876. However, few of his suggestions were to be adopted. There were good reasons why the pilotage charges to Exeter should be much higher than those levied for the north-east ports. The Exe estuary was both narrow and tortuous, making if far more difficult and time-consuming to navigate. Similarly, the town dues were a legitimate charge for the use of the inland port and formed a source of income that neither the city council nor the canal creditors could afford to lose.

Some improvements were made, the South Devon Railway at long last approving the use of the standard gauge line from the canal basin to St David's station in October 1876. Steam power was allowed on the canal more than three years later, the navigation committee agreeing to this as an experiment in January 1880. The ship selected, the S.S. *Ossian,* was allowed to travel to Exeter quay under her own power, the canal surveyor superintending the passage. The experiment was successful and the *Ossian* became a regular visitor to the quay, laden with cargoes of wine. At first steam towage was prohibited for fear of damage to the banks. Then, in September 1880, the city council accepted the offer of a Mr. Nobbs, owner of an 8 h.p. steam launch, to tow a ship up the canal from Turf. The *Majesticus,* laden with 360 tons of coal and drawing 12ft. 4in., was selected and once again the experiment was successful. Thereafter steam towage was permitted. It had been undertaken from the mouth of the Exe estuary to Turf lock from the 1840s, though there were periods when this facility was not available. They usually occurred on the withdrawal of the tug by one private owner and its replacement by another.[15]

The major repairs itemised in William Beardmore's report of 1867 had been carried out at Turf lock and King's Arms sluice. To avoid a heavy strain on the already much reduced canal income, the canal creditors had agreed to a temporary loan being raised on each occasion to meet the costs involved. The money was borrowed from the corporation's bankers, repayment being spread over a period of several years.

By 1880 the need for new gates at Double locks had become critical and repairs were put in hand. The canal creditors were not consulted about them, the city council considering them to be 'ordinary' repairs within the terms of the 1857 Deed of Arrangement. Indeed, the two lots of major repairs at Turf lock and King's Arms sluice had been treated in a similar fashion without any objection being raised. On this occasion, too, the receiver of the canal creditors paid one-third of the cost without comment. Trouble came when the city council suggested that the remainder be raised by a temporary loan, as had occurred in the past. The canal creditors strongly objected, considering that they should have given their prior consent to what they deemed to be 'extraordinary' repairs within the terms of the Deed of Arrangement.[16]

The reason for this hostile action was that for many years the canal creditors had been receiving less than 2 per cent. interest on their mortgages instead of the expected 4½ per cent. The dramatic fall in income, owing to competition from the railways, had been compounded by the actions of the city council. As already mentioned, when the statutory mortgages of £34,500 had been redeemed in 1866, the corporation had rearranged its income to ensure that there was no surplus which could be paid to the receiver for the canal creditors. Furthermore, not only were the canal creditors bearing the cost of major repairs to the waterway, but also paying interest on the temporary loans already negotiated. If they agreed to a further loan for Double locks it was most likely that the interest payable on their mortgages would be even further reduced.

The town clerk, Bartholomew C. Gidley, advised the city council that the claim of the canal creditors to control the expenditure on Double locks was untenable. He stated that:

> . . . fitting new gates to a lock is unquestionably a repair to that Lock and to the Canal of which it forms a vital part, and although, happily, the necessity for new gates arises only at long intervals of time, yet, nevertheless, they are not on that account to be called extraordinary, but must be considered as much ordinary repairs as would be the substitution of new Sleepers and Rails in the maintenance of the permanent way of a railway.

He also considered that the provision for the payment of surplus income from the corporate property, other than the canal, to the receiver for the canal creditors had ceased to have effect once the statutory mortgages had been repaid.[17]

The canal creditors sought legal opinion on the town clerk's advice and had the satisfaction of finding that their contentions were upheld. Thereafter the stranglehold on the canal finances became even tighter. A crisis was reached in January 1882 when the coaster *Mary*, drawing 11ft. 4in., was stuck in the entrance channel leading to Turf lock. The cause was the lack of dredging and when the town clerk asked the canal creditors to agree to the silt being removed his request was refused. The city council then decided to take steps to regain control of the canal.[18]

After discussions with the canal creditors the city council reached an agreement. The proposed terms of settlement were that the corporation should pay £25 per cent. to the canal creditors in settlement of their outstanding capital debt of £51,550. Of the £950 held by the receiver, £500 was to be retained to cover the

CITY & COUNTY OF THE CITY OF EXETER.

Municipal Corporations (Borough Funds) Act, 1872.

To the Right Worshipful the Mayor of Exeter,
(THOMAS ANDREW, ESQUIRE.)

WE, the undersigned, being either Ratepayers, or Owners resident in the District of the City and County of the City of Exeter, hereby request you to summon

A MEETING

of Owners and Ratepayers, under the Municipal Corporations (Borough Funds) Act, 1872, for the purpose of considering, and (if so determined) of consenting to, the proposal of the Town Council to promote a Bill in the next ensuing Session of Parliament enabling the Corporation of Exeter to redeem the outstanding Canal Statutory Mortgages and to raise money.

Dated 19th July, 1882.

W. J. Richards, Terrace House, Exeter
Chas. T. K. Roberts, 29, St. Leonard-road
Samuel Jones, 12, Longbrook-street
William Pidsley, 42, Catherine-street
William Peters, Palace-gate
R. Southcott, 26, Southernhay West, Exeter
William Wreford, 15, Belmont-road, Exeter
W. Buckingham, 12, Southernhay

Henry S. Eland, High-street
Geo. Wippell, 231 and 232, High-street,
Walter Friend, Devonshire-place
Henry D. Thomas, 9, Dix's-field
Thomas Rowe, Pennsylvania
James Pearse, St. David's-hill
R. C. Wilkinson, 150, Fore-street
Charles Westron, 6, Elmgrove-road
Henry Wilcocks, Spurharne

Morris Hart, Fore-street
W. S. Pasmore, Victoria Villa, Pennsylvania
Edward Peters, Palace-gate
James Courtney, Bartholomew-terrace
William Huxtable, The Mint
Henry Hexter, Queen-street
Edward Knapman, 206 and 207, High-street

Pursuant to the foregoing Requisition, I the undersigned THOMAS ANDREW, Mayor of Exeter, hereby convene a Meeting of Owners and Ratepayers of the City and County of the City of Exeter, at the

GUILDHALL, on FRIDAY, the 28th day of this instant, month of July, at 3 o'Clock in the Afternoon precisely.

THOMAS ANDREW, Mayor.

Dated July 21st, 1882.

Figure 13.   Notice of meeting about the canal mortgages.

costs and expenses of the canal creditors and the remaining £450 returned to the city council on the ultimate settlement of the outstanding debt. It was further agreed that the city council would meet the cost of repairs to Double locks. Subject to the approval of the owners of three-fourths in value of the mortgages, the corporation would promote a Bill in the next session of parliament to carry the arrangement into effect. The promotion costs would be met by the corporation and, until the Royal Assent had been given to the Act, the receivership of the canal income should continue. During this interim period the city council would be at liberty to carry out any dredging or repairs they considered necessary though, if for any reason, the proposed arrangement did not come into effect the understanding about dredging and repairs should become void.[19]

Both the canal creditors and the city council agreed that a public meeting should be called to discuss the proposed terms of settlement (*see* opposite). This was held at the Guildhall, Exeter, on Friday, 28 July 1882, when the arrangement received general approval. On 18 June 1883 'An Act for sanctioning a settlement of the claims of the Mortgagees of the Exeter Canal against the Corporation of the City of Exeter' received the Royal Assent. At long last the canal was free from outside control, though the chief clerk, Richard Banfill, was not able to share in the relief as he died on 1 May 1883 after 60 years of service.[20]

Although the canal remained a profitable asset, there were troublesome times ahead as the city council fought to regain some of the loss in trade.

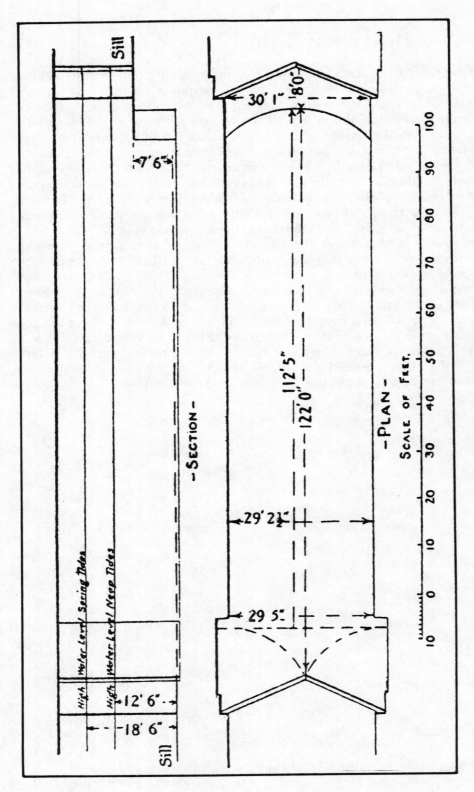

Figure 14. Plan of Turf lock.

Chapter Seven

DECADES OF DECLINE (1884–1963)

TRADE HAD SUFFERED an almost continuous period of decline during the administration of the receiver for the canal creditors. One of the first actions of the city council, when they regained control of the canal, was to consider ways of halting this decline. A sub-committee was formed and reported in 1884 that a major cause of the loss of trade was the high rate of tolls and dues. Unless these were 'materially reduced' they considered the decline would continue. Their advice was accepted and the rates cut to about one-third of those formerly charged.[1]

It was decided to abandon the contract for horse towage after Michaelmas 1884, the navigation committee spending £330 on the purchase of the small steam tug *Exonia*. Built by Norris of Belfast in 1891, she was 30ft. long and had a 9ft. beam and 4ft. 6in. draught. Estimates showed that the costs of maintenance, depreciation, wages, repairs, etc., would be £260 per annum, compared with the £345 then being spent on horse towage contract. These estimates were grossly inaccurate, as the committee were to find out when the *Exonia* had been at work for some months.[2]

Another change was the discontinuance of the dredging contract, and a steam grab dredger was ordered from Rose, Downs & Thompson of Hull. In January 1884 the navigation committee was informed that the dredger had nearly paid its first cost in some 18 months' operation, compared with the price formerly paid for contract dredging. Steam towage was not as successful, a deficit occurring each year. The following returns are based on the year ending at Michaelmas:

Year	Receipts	Payments	Deficit	Notes
1882-83	£266	£345	£79	Towage by horses
1883-84	£259	£345	£84	Towage by horses
1884-85	£249	£442	£193	Towage by tug
1885-86	£287	£434	£147	Towage by tug

The committee suggested in January 1887 that the canal should revert to horse towage, to be undertaken by the city council and not let out to contract. In October of that year it was decided to sell the *Exonia*.[3]

Steam towage between the mouth of the Exe estuary and Turf lock had been provided by a number of private operators since the 1840s. When the existing tug was withdrawn and sold in 1884 there was concern that the recently rebuilt

Exmouth dock might benefit through increased trade, owing to the lack of a replacement tug. The city council rose to the challenge in 1886 and purchased the tug *Telephone,* replacing it later that year by the *Queen of the Exe.* The latter continued in service until 1913, a time when the era of the sailing ship was coming to an end.[4]

Plans for an expensive tidal basin at Turf were rejected by the traders in 1886, though it was claimed that larger ships would then be able to unload their cargoes into lighters in calm waters. Instead, the traders were far more concerned about the continual delays in access to the quay at Exeter. Whenever there was unusually wet weather the gates at King's Arms sluice were closed, preventing passage. There were complaints, too, about the lack of horse towage, and in 1894 the owners of the *James Simpson* claimed £15 for unnecessary delays at Turf lock. This claim was rejected, the navigation committee commenting 'with regard to the claim for detention at Turf the Council are under no obligation to provide horses for towing vessels through the Canal'.[5]

Despite the occasional lack of horse towage, efforts to gain more trade were gradually successful. The tonnage carried upon the canal increased from 30,514 tons in 1888 to 50,442 tons in 1898, with a corresponding increase in revenue from £1,950 to £2,200. There was little change in the direction of trade, with less than 10 per cent. destined for export (4,267 tons in 1898). At that time the imports were recorded as coal, soft fish, oil cake, oil, stone, sugar, timber, wines and spirits. The exports were barytes (used for making white paint and wallpaper) and timber.[6]

Though encouraging trade, the navigation committee were not so keen on pleasure traffic and refused the application of Mr. J. E. Thomas, a consulting engineer, who wanted to run trips on the canal. He had a 22-ft. long clinker-built launch with a 2 h.p. engine and planned to use this for excursions from the quay, Double locks and Turf between 5 p.m. and 9 p.m. during the period from May to September 1894.[7]

The proposals to extend Turf lock were revived in 1895, after the secretary of the Exeter Gas Light and Coke Co. had written to the navigation committee. He wished to know if it was their intention to extend the locks, as it would enable his company and merchants generally to bring ships of double the present capacity to the city. The canal surveyor was asked in January to prepare a report and this was ready in September. The estimated cost of lengthening Turf lock and straightening out the canal bends was £6,000, the job taking six months to complete. The committee decided in October to take no further action.[8]

However, an application by the Missions to Seamen to erect an iron building 30ft. long, 15ft. 6ins. wide and 12ft. high at Exeter basin was approved at an annual tenancy of 1s. 0d. It was to be used 'as a Reading and Recreation Room and for Religious Services by Sailors using the Port'. There was also a more benevolent attitude to pleasure craft from 1908, it being decided to issue a licence for motor boats at an annual fee of 5s. 0d.[9]

The steady revival of trade during the latter years of the 19th century was to be short lived. In 1908 a canal committee was appointed by the city council:

... to consider the present serious position of our mercantile trade, and how facilities can be given to improve our navigation. Furthermore, that an estimate be obtained for bringing the Canal up-to-date so that it may accommodate the ordinary coasting steamer of about 800 tons and not more than 1,000.

Their report was presented to the city council in September, recommending that the canal be widened to take craft of up to 200ft. length, 30ft. beam and 14ft. draught. They considered that Turf lock should be at least 210ft. long and 36ft. wide, and that all bridges and lock gates (except at Topsham) should be of the same width. Some curves would need straightening to permit a 200ft.-long ship to navigate the canal, and a new steam dredger was also required.[10]

The city council asked their engineer and surveyor, Thomas Moulding, to make estimates of the costs involved. In May 1909 he was asked to prepare modified figures on the basis that the largest ship to use the canal would be one of 500 tons. Moulding's report of 20 October recommended the purchase of a bucket dredger and two hopper barges for £2,600. The four largest craft then using the waterway had draughts of between 13ft. and 13ft. 6in., the greatest length being 114ft. 6in., and the greatest beam 24ft. 4in. All of these ships had to be lightened by between 40 to 75 tons at Turf to reduce the draught to 12ft. 6in. Even at this reduced draught they still stirred up the mud on the bottom of the canal bed, though the original depth of the waterway was 15 feet. To dredge to this depth, and to the minimum width of 12 feet at the bottom, would require the removal of 175,000 tons of mud. This would then permit steamships of 250 tons to use the canal.

If the size of the craft was to be increased to 500 tons, Turf lock would need lengthening, bridges widened, several curves eased, and a turning place made at the basin in Exeter. The total cost of these alterations was estimated at £49,000. None of them was undertaken. The navigation committee resolved in March 1910 'that in view of the great expenditure required and the absence of any reasonable prospect of increase in trade the Committee are unable to recommend improvements'.[11]

Between 1901-10 an average of 275 craft a year were using the canal for trade. In addition there were 94 pleasure boats and a motor boat which was licensed to ply for hire in 1910, a trip along the waterway being a favourite Sunday afternoon outing. The annual report for that year referred to the upper gates of Double locks, which 'required considerable repairs or renewal at an early date'. The existing gates were put in during 1881 and the cost of new ones would be £750, or £350 if repairs alone were made. The latter course of action was chosen but, on closer examination, it was found that the woodwork of the upper gates was so rotten that it needed complete renewal. The canal was closed for six weeks and four days whilst the repairs were made, re-opening on 4 December 1911.[12]

There was a further stoppage in July 1915, this time to repair the leaking upper gates of Turf lock. The work took a month and cost £437. It had little effect in arresting the declining trade as canal traffic had fallen rapidly since the outbreak of World War I and, in May 1916, the navigation committee decided that there was no longer a need to keep a horse stabled at Turf for towage purposes. The animal was moved from its lonely outpost to the city stables.[13]

When World War I ended there were thoughts of buying another canal tug, since the *Queen of the Exe* had been sold in 1913. The city surveyor was asked to make enquiries, though later it was resolved to postpone the purchase indefinitely as 'the provision of a tug would effect very little improvement in canal traffic'. A new bridge at Countess Wear was agreed to, and Orr Watt & Co. Ltd. of Motherwell had their tender of £686 for this structure accepted by the navigation committee at their August 1922 meeting.[14]

The long period of neglect resulting from World War I caused many delays, and the captains of several ships threatened that they would not come again to Exeter unless improvements were made. The decline in trade had been so great that the canal was now losing £1,000 a year. The navigation committee discussed what could be done to improve matters and, once again, the lengthening of Turf lock was discussed. They resolved to take no action over this, but recommended the purchase of a new tug at a cost not exceeding £1,500. They also proposed the appointment of a wharfinger and the purchase of a new dredger and three hopper barges, proposals which caused animated discussion when the city council met on 28 May 1924.[15]

Since the sale of the *Queen of the Exe* any ships needing to be towed up the canal had to use horse towage. From May 1916 onwards, towing facilities were provided by the Teignmouth Tug Company. There were the inevitable complaints if the Teignmouth tug was needed for other purposes or out of action. Some councillors objected to the proposed purchase of a 100 h.p. tug, one claiming that 'our canal is an excellent place for rowing boats, but it will be of no use to the trade of the city'. Another observed 'you cannot resuscitate trade over the canal. The monument of your difficulties is in your empty warehouses on the quay'. Yet a third urged that the canal be allowed to remain as at present, or else sold as a swimming bath.

One reason for the declining trade was the lack of dredging. There was an accumulation of over 90,000 tons of silt awaiting removal and it was said that, if the city council did not at once begin drastic methods of dredging, they might as well close the port. The proposals of the navigation committee for the purchase of a tug and dredger were then approved, the city council having been assured that the canal was of definite value to the trade of the city. The lengthening of Turf lock was also discussed, the city surveyor estimating it would cost £10,000 to extend it a further 30 feet, and so make it possible for a 500-ton ship to navigate from the mouth of the Exe estuary to Exeter on a three-quarter tide. He was then asked to prepare a report on this subject.

Another discussion on Turf lock took place at the navigation committee meeting in June 1924. The city surveyor had calculated that £20,000 would be required to extend it a further 50 feet, and it was again resolved that no action be taken. In September the tug *Venture III* was purchased for £1,260, and in

February 1925 a dredger and two hopper barges bought for £6,800. Further expense was caused in midsummer when the apron of the tail gates cracked at Turf lock. A major repair became necessary when water continued to enter the lock pit after it had been drained, the cost amounting to £5,100.[16]

The growth of road transport after the end of World War I brought an increasing demand for petrol, and the establishment of two storage depots near the canal basin at Exeter gained new trade by the end of the 1920s. This came too late to stop the sale of the canal tug *Venture III,* whose disposal in June 1928 for £300 was 'owing to slackness of trade'. Captain C. W. Lamphrey, lock-keeper at Double locks, had also suffered a loss of trade at his hotel and asked for an increase in his present £100 per annum salary. This request was refused, a grant of £50 being made:

> . . . having regard to the fact that the business of the hotel has declined on account of the cheap evening excursions run by the Railway Companies during the summer season.[17]

The main imports, apart from petroleum, were now coal, timber, cement and sugar. The petroleum trade received an added boost in 1933 when Trinidad Leaseholds acquired land near the canal basin for development as a storage depot with a capacity of 234,000 gallons. The navigation committee agreed to provide a wharf for an additional payment of £400, with £100 per annum thereafter for a period of 14 years. It was intended that three tankers per month would bring supplies to the depot. Although the import trade was now increasing there was virtually no export trade, all but a handful of the ships using the port having to return empty in ballast.[18]

To encourage trade the navigation committee arranged for two men on bicycles to conduct each ship to and from Turf lock, this service being provided free of charge. At the beginning of 1934 the lock-keepers' salaries were increased. W. B. Tupper, lock-keeper at Turf, was given £18 more, raising his pay to £104 per annum. Captain C. W. Lamphrey, who served as harbourmaster and wharfinger in addition to his duties at Double locks, had his wharfinger's salary increased by £25, making his total pay £175 per annum.[19]

December 1934 was an exceptionally rainy month. The *Seine,* laden with sugar from London, reached the quay at Exeter on the last day of November and had to remain there until 4 January because the river was too high to allow re-entry into the canal through King's Arms sluice. She then went down the waterway in the company of four other ships, passing the cut leading to the basin at about 10 a.m. The others were the tankers *William Kipping* and *Ben Johnson,* together with the *Quo Vadis* and *Welcome* which had both carried sugar to Exeter. They were all passed through Double and Turf locks in record time, being clear of the canal by 3.50 p.m., 1½ hours before high tide.[20]

Whilst the *Seine* was detained at Exeter quay by floodwaters there was an incident at Countess Wear swing-bridge. The coaster *Aqueity,* laden with 300 tons of coal for Exeter gas works, passed through Turf locks on 20 December and then became stuck at the bridge. She was freed when parts of her side plates were cut away. The manoeuvre caused severe dislocation to road traffic, the swing-bridge having to remain open to the canal. The same year the *Quo Vadis,* already mentioned above, came into the port with a 400-ton load of timber.[21]

Not long after the incident at Countess Wear it was decided that the existing narrow bridge should be replaced by an electrically-operated one built of steel. This had a 20ft.-wide central carriage way and a 5ft.-wide footway, being 107ft. long. It was commissioned by Devon County Council because the present bridge was inadequate for the traffic demands of the Exeter by-pass, and completed by Horsley Bridge and Thomas Piggott Ltd. of Tipton, Staffs., on 2 March 1937.[22]

Larger ships using the canal had insufficient room to turn in the canal basin at Exeter. The normal practice was to enter the river through King's Arms sluice and turn there, though in times of flood a ship had to proceed stern first to the site of Matford limekilns, beyond Countess Wear, where was room to turn in the canal. In the autum 1937 the basin was widened to 125 feet by the canal maintenance staff at a cost of £1,086. Double locks hotel was provided with an electricity supply for the first time, and a motor barge was purchased for the use of the canal staff. Previously all materials needed for maintenance work had to be loaded into dumb barges and towed along the canal by horses.[23]

The volume of shipping continued to increase during the 1930s. Figures given below are for the four years ending on 31 March 1938:

Year	1935	1936	1937	1938
INWARD craft	237	253	248	238
Cargo (tons)	40,693	46,446	48,392	50,390
OUTWARD craft	10	11	2	38
Cargo (tons)	2,400	2,158	451	7,165

This period of success was not to be enjoyed for much longer. The outbreak of World War II in September 1939 immediately brought a drop in trade. Captain Lamphrey did not live to see the havoc brought by the war, having died on 27 October 1938. After his death it was decided by the navigation committee to separate the jobs of harbourmaster and wharfinger from that of lock-keeper at Double locks.[24]

One immediate effect of the war was the suspension of horse towage. Another was that commercial trade virtually ceased, apart from small tankers delivering petrol. During the 'blitz' of 1942 several bombs fell in or near to the canal, one causing a direct hit on the wall of the basin at Exeter and another damaging the canal superintendent's accommodation. Many of the small coasters which had used the canal in peace-time were sunk by enemy action, or else had received such severe damage that they were beyond economic repair. In consequence, trade was slow to pick up again when the war ended. Only 46 ships entered the port of Exeter in 1945, though the number increased the following year. By 1948 there were 145 ships using the canal, their cargoes totalling 31,132 tons plus 936 standards of timber.[25]

The lock-keepers' premises at Topsham and Double locks now received a few modern comforts, Topsham lock being provided with a water and electricity supply in 1947, and Double locks having a connection made with the public water supply in 1948. Because of the increase in volume of shipping the canal foreman was provided with a 125 c.c. motor cycle, speeding journeys between Turf lock and the city basin formerly made by bicycle.[26]

The town clerk produced correspondence from some of the traders at the meeting of the navigation committee in June 1950. They had pointed out that the small ships using the canal were becoming old and unreliable and were uneconomical to replace in their present size. They asked the city council to consider extending Turf lock and improving the waterway to allow larger craft to trade to the city basin. The city surveyor was then asked to prepare a paper on the subject.[27]

The city surveyor informed the navigation committee in November that it was currently possible to admit ships of 122ft. length, 29ft. beam and 11ft. 6in. draught, which gave an average cargo capacity of 250 tons, though specially designed ships could carry as much as 350 tons. The width of Turf lock was ample for craft up to 180ft. long and the minimum draught throughout the canal in summer months was 10ft. 6in. Restrictions at Double locks and other parts of the canal limited the maximum beam beyond Countess Wear swing-bridge to 25ft. 6in. For ships trading to the basin the governing dimensions were therefore 25ft. 6in. beam, which usually went with craft of up to 160ft. length carrying 350/400 tons of cargo. A new turning space was being made at the basin which, with small improvements above the swing-bridge at Countess Wear, would ease the passage of these larger vessels. Wider-beam ships could not be accommodated unless the canal was completely reconstructed, and this could not be considered.

The constructional problem was therefore to add 40 feet to Turf lock at the least cost with the least inconvenience to shipping. To lengthen the lock inwards would entail the complete closure of the canal and the expensive underpinning of the existing masonry walls. If the lock was extended in the seawards direction, it might be possible to carry out much of the work behind temporary dams without closing the canal to shipping. The extension would bring the lock out into tidal waters where a base would have to be found for the 25-ft. high retaining walls, strong enough to withstand water and earth pressure and the thrust of the gates when closed and retaining water. These difficulties were compounded by the lack of road access and the problem of finding a firm bottom at a reasonable depth.

Having explained these snags to the navigation committee, the city surveyor recommended that money be provided in the financial estimates for an investigation to be made of the sub-strata below the proposed extension, both inwards and outwards. Without this knowledge it was impracticable to make an estimate of the cost. The committee agreed and recommended that £750 be appropriated for that purpose.

The exploratory drilling was carried out in 1951 and showed that there was firm gravel 8 feet to 10 feet below the mud level, and red rock 25 feet below that level. The city surveyor was then asked to prepare a survey of the canal and a design for extending Turf lock, with estimates of the cost. He was also to contact the appropriate shipping companies, to see what increase in trade could be expected if the lock were to be extended.[28]

The early 1950s saw a steady increase in trade, the main imports being petrol, cement and timber. The growth in the last two trades was brought about by the post-war construction boom, particularly in housing. By 1953 the cargoes were becoming more varied, with animal feeding stuffs arriving from continental ports, and oats from Scotland, the latter a trade that had formerly gone by rail. After an absence of many years the coal trade also resumed, the first cargo being unloaded just before the end of the year.[29]

Besides preparing plans for the extension to Turf, the city surveyor was also involved with war damage repairs to the city basin. Owing to the increase in shipping it was decided that the restoration should only be carried out during normal periods of maintenance, starting in November 1951. The new wall was built some 50 feet behind the old one, to allow ships of up to 160 feet in length to turn in the basin, the work being undertaken by the canal maintenance staff.[30]

The adaptability of the maintenance staff is exemplified by another incident on Wednesday, 13 August 1952, when the tanker *Ben Johnson* was approaching Countess Wear. As the bridge was being swung at 1.30 p.m. the main driving shaft snapped, jamming it in a partly open position. Neither ship nor cars could pass as the bridge was immovable until the damaged parts could be lifted out by a mobile crane. It was then opened and closed with winches and tractors during the whole of Thursday and Friday morning, to allow both canal and road traffic to pass unhindered. By 7 a.m. on Saturday a replacement part had been made and fitted, and the bridge could once more be electrically operated. The navigation committee were so impressed by the speed and initiative of the canal foreman and his staff that they recorded their appreciation in the minutes of their next meeting.[31]

In 1953 the city surveyor calculated that the cost of extending Turf lock and carrying out other improvements, so that larger ships could use the canal, would be in the region of £150,000. None of the major traders would commit themselves on the future use of the waterway. Instead, in 1954 the shipping manager of Shell-Mex & B.P. said that it was his company's intention to supply their Exminster depot by road from Bridgwater. The navigation committee decided to take no further action on the proposals for the Turf lock extension.[32]

During the 1880s there used to be regular inspections of the canal by the city council and invited guests. A revival of this custom took place in 1953 and continued in 1954. On the latter occasion members of the Exeter Port Health Authority boarded the open launch *Reliance* for the journey through the canal and across the estuary to Exmouth. In 1955 repairs were made to Double locks, new balance beams being fitted to the outer gates. Each had a plaque which read:

This beam is formed of part of the FOREMAST of H.M.S. EXETER.
After the cruiser was refitted at Devonport following action in the
Battle of the River Plate in December, 1940, this Foremast was given
to the City of Exeter by the Lords Commissioners of the Admiralty.
The cruiser was later sunk in the Battle of the Java Sea in February
1942.[33]

The year ending 31 March 1956 saw an increase of 10 per cent. on the previous
year's traffic, with 63,258 tons passing through the port in what was to be the
peak year for post-war trade. Of the 296 ships using the port, 223 brought motor
spirit, 42 cement, 13 timber, and the remaining 18 had miscellaneous cargoes of
oyster shells, oats, general stores, sugar and flour. Coal, once the mainstay of
the canal, was down to two loads, and this trade ceased entirely in June 1955.
The year was not without incident, the tanker *Ben Johnson* damaging the outer
gates of Turf lock on the afternoon of 9 December. Once again the maintenance
staff came to the rescue and almost non-stop work by the canal foreman and his
gang brought the stoppage to a speedy conclusion.[34]

From 1958 onwards motor spirit provided more than 90 per cent. of the trade,
timber making most of the remainder. The import of cement ceased that year in
favour of road transport, and the petroleum trade, too, was soon to be threatened.
Both Regent and National Benzole gave notice that they would be ceasing to
convey supplies to their depots by coastal tankers. There had been some minor
improvements to the canal structures, Turf lock receiving its first electricity
supply when a diesel 2¼ k.w. alternator generator was installed in 1957. About
this time the old limekilns, adjoining the canal bank below Countess Wear swing-
bridge, were removed by the use of explosives. In 1960 facilities for the laying-up
of small boats were offered at land adjoining the city basin, a 10-ton crane being
available to lift them out of the water. To aid ships waiting to enter Turf lock a
steel mast with a sliding orange disc was erected in 1962, this showing when
traffic could proceed.[35]

The 'big freeze' of 1962–63 caused the closure of the canal from 10 January
until 18 February due to 5-in. thick ice. Both Turf and Double locks were frozen,
though no damage was caused to the gates. A more permanent loss of traffic was
the withdrawal of the oil tanker trade of the Regent and National Benzole
companies, causing the tonnage to slump from 49,000 tons in 1962–63 to
25,959 tons in 1963–64. There was one new ship on the canal, the city council's
own *SW2*. She was a 122-ft. long sludge vessel, operated by a crew of five, and
built as part of the scheme for the reconstruction of Countess Wear sewage works.
The ship had a single screw and the turbo-charge propulsion engine gave a speed
of 5 knots when fully laden with 350 tons of liquid sewage. Pumps could
discharge this sludge in a half hour in the sea outside the 5-mile limit. Sea trials
from Bolson's Yard, Poole, were completed in March and she came into service
on 27 May 1963.[36]

In the year ending 31 March 1964 the *SW2* made 132 voyages carrying a total
of 33,848 tons of sludge. Her main berth was alongside the Countess Wear sewage
works, extensive dredging having been made at this point. The strange name of

the ship was simply a code abbreviation for 'Sewage Works No. 2', SW1 being the works lorry, whilst SW3 was said to be the foreman's bicycle![37]

With trade down to almost half of its previous level, by the end of March 1964 the navigation committee became very concerned about the increasing financial liability. The city engineer and surveyor was asked to carry out an investigation into the future of the canal and to prepare a report on the subject with the aid of the city treasurer. The future looked bleak.

Chapter Eight

SAILING TO SUCCESS (1964 onwards)

THE REPORT *Investigation into the Future of the Canal* was completed in November 1964 by the City Engineer & Surveyor, Mr. J. Brierley, and the City Treasurer, Mr. H. C. Haley. Three courses of action were considered:

1. The retention of the canal for shipping.
2. Closure to shipping, but retention as a waterway.
3. Complete closure and draining.

The report showed that the tonnage had fallen from 55,431 in 277 ships during the year 1960-61 to 25,959 in 120 ships in 1963-64. The deficit had correspondingly increased from £7,335 in 1960-61 to an estimated £22,921 for 1964-65. Admittedly the figure for the current year was exceptionally high, as it included special repair work following an underwater survey. However, in future years the deficit was estimated to be £10,000 to £12,000 per annum.

The alternatives to an annual charge of £12,000 on the rates were:

(a)	Closing the entire canal but retaining it in water	£21,000
(b)	Closing the upper part of the canal from Double locks and retaining it in water	£15,300
(c)	Closing the entire canal and draining it	£9,150
(d)	Closing the upper part of the canal from Double locks and draining it	£10,425

The report recommended that the canal be kept open for shipping. The navigation committee agreed and resolved 'that no decision be taken at the present time' on the future of the Exeter Canal.[1]

One reason why further consideration was deferred was that informal discussions were then in progress with Major David Goddard, an army officer who had plans for a maritime museum centred on the canal. He wanted to form an international sailcraft association to develop the quay warehouses and city basin as a museum for working craft from all over the world. His plans envisaged a marina for sailing enthusiasts coming up the waterway from the sea, a restaurant, shops and boating facilities. The estimated cost of running the museum was £40,000 a year, though it would become self-supporting from the income it would earn such as entrance fees, etc., and become an important new holiday attraction. The council's finance committee asked for more details.[2]

The idea of a maritime museum did not meet with universal approval and the small boat owners who used the laying-up facilities at the city basin were virulent in their opposition. Another plan for the canal was produced by a retired surveyor from Pinhoe, Mr. Frank Baker. He suggested enlarging it between Turf lock and Countess Wear and constructing a new basin south of the swing-bridge, so that this length could take sea-going ships of between 450–600 tons. The remainder would then be filled in. The alterations were estimated to cost about £1 million.[3]

In October 1966 Mr. Baker revised his plans, now suggesting that the only section to be filled in should be that between Countess Wear and Double lock. It was still proposed to convert this length into a road for heavy commercial vehicles serving the Marsh Barton industrial estate. The length from Double locks to the city basin would be retained for amenity purposes. Though there had been some support within Exeter for Mr. Baker's earlier scheme, the city council were reminded at their meeting of 29 September that the sludge vessel *SW2* was a user of the canal. If the waterway were to be closed the city would have to consider new sewage works. Other regular users were Esso Petroleum, who had a 14-year lease on canal-side property from 25 December 1956, and the timber merchants, Gabriel Wade & English Ltd. These observations effectively put an end to Mr. Baker's plans.[4]

Discussion about the waterway was aired in the local press on several occasions. Many correspondents were concerned at the ever-increasing losses borne by the city ratepayers (in the three years ending in September 1966 about £75,000 was spent on the canal). Letters in favour of its continued existence were fewer, though an outstanding contribution was made by Mr. Frederick Smith of St Luke's College, Exeter, who wrote in October 1966:

> . . . the Cathedral, in the strictest commercial sense, does not pay its way, but there is no suggestion that we might as well let the roof fall in on the grounds that there are other churches people can go to. The Cathedral is part of Exeter's heritage. So is the canal.[5]

Mr. Smith's letter had not been written in vain. Members of the navigation committee were told at their meeting on 29 November that the city council had agreed to support the proposed maritime museum. They had passed no resolution on the future of the canal, preferring to wait for the opinion of the committee. The Deputy Surveyor, Mr. A. W. Thompson, reminded those present that the 1964 report had showed that it was cheaper to keep the canal open. In any event, it could not be closed until the Esso Petroleum lease expired at the end of 1970. The company had said they had no immediate plans to change the method of supply to their Exeter Depot.[6]

When questioned about the decreased use of the canal during the year, Mr. Thompson explained it had been closed for four months whilst new inner gates were fitted at Double locks. These cost £15,711. His report showed a continued decline in commercial traffic, with tonnage falling to 19,268 in 1965–66. Of the 86 ships using the waterway, all but 10 were laden with motor spirit. Eight of the others carried timber, and the remaining two had cargoes of oyster shells.

He considered that 'so long as motor spirit came up the canal it was worthwhile keeping things as they were'.[7]

The previous year a new steel-sectioned dredger pontoon had been constructed for the navigation committee. It was built to accommodate an R.B.10 excavator with dredger bucket, so that it could dredge from the centre of the canal. That same year the sludge vessel *SW2* had been purchased by the city council for £95,000. In July 1966 the city council made their annual inspection, chartering the pleasure boat *Devon Princess* for the voyage from the city basin to Turf lock and across the Exe estuary to Exmouth.[8]

From 1 January 1967 it was decided to combine the duties of wharfinger and harbourmaster with those of canal superintendent. The navigation committee were never to take a decision about the future of the canal, holding their final meeting on 4 April 1967. Under a reorganisation by the city council, the navigation committee was amalgamated with the public works and traffic management committees from June 1967. It fell to this new committee to deal with the 50-ft. breach in the western canal bank, about half a mile south of Topsham lock. This occurred during the night of 13–14 August and lowered the water level to 8 feet, flooding low-lying meadowland. The repair took several weeks, needing about 4,000 tons of clay hogging to stabilise the banks, and cost £17,000.[9]

The breach was one of several factors that had affected the canal since the 1964 report on its future had been prepared. The ever-increasing deficit (equal to the product of a ½d. rate in 1966) caused continued concern. Other factors were the extension of the M5 motorway, which was planned to cross the canal near Countess Wear sewage works, the maritime museum, and the amenity aspects of the immediate area. The latter had not been considered in the 1964 report, though it was when the committee called for a comprehensive survey of the canal and the future financial implications involved.

Whilst the report was being prepared the maritime museum was taking shape, aided by grants of £3,000 from the city council who also provided warehouses to house the exhibits. Equally generous aid was given by shipping companies, the armed services and airlines who transported exhibits without charge. About £2,000 was raised by public subscription, another £1,000 being contributed by the director designate, Mr. Goddard. He also helped to purchase one of the showpieces, the 310-ton Danish steam tug *St Canute*, built in 1931 as a harbour tug and icebreaker for Odense, and later used by Fowey Harbour Commissioners.[10]

On 27 June 1969 the Exeter Maritime Museum was officially opened by round-the-world yachtsman, Sir Alec Rose. At first there were 23 different craft on view. The number has since grown rapidly; the Ocean Rowers Collection was opened on 1 April 1975 by Chay Blyth, and the Ellerman Collection of Portuguese working craft later the same year by the Portuguese ambassador. There are now over 100 craft at the city basin or the quay warehouse.[11]

In November 1969 two reports were produced. The first, *A further consideration of the future of the Exeter Canal,* had been prepared by the city engineer & surveyor, city treasurer and town clerk, and set out the financial implications. Dealing with the M5 motorway, it noted 'when work begins the use of the Exeter

Canal as a commercial waterway will effectively cease'. The city council had asked that the motorway viaduct across the canal be built at a height of 80 feet, but the Ministry of Transport ruled that it would have to be 30 feet on grounds of cost. This put an end to the economic operation of commercial shipping though, by fitting a telescopic mast, the city council's sludge vessel *SW2* would clear the viaduct.

The canal was much used for walking, fishing and boating, but there had been no attempt to cater for amenity aspects with landing stages, picnic sites, etc. The report noted that 82 private craft and 23 excursion vessels had used the canal in 1968. A visual survey of the banks had shown they were relatively safe except for the top 3 feet to 4 feet, and the upper portion of the west bank from Topsham to Turf was considered unsatisfactory. It was recommended that an additional £10,000 per annum be included in the estimates to allow a programme of improvement, starting from Turf, and that a stock of sheet piling be kept for use in an emergency.

Of the lock gates, only the inner ones at Double locks were new and in good condition. At least four other pairs were in need of repair or renewal at a cost of at least £20,000 a pair. The report recommended that £80,000 be allowed for this in a capital expenditure programme. Some repointing or grouting was constantly required at the lock pits, adding a further £1,000 a year to the estimates. The two wooden swing-bridges at the city basin were coming to the end of their working life, as was the one at Topsham. A further £20,000 should be allowed for in the capital expenditure to cover replacement costs.

Disregarding the capital expenditure programme of £100,000, and the additional £11,000 to be added to the canal estimates each year until it was brought into a satisfactory condition, the deficit for 1969–70 was estimated to be £14,170. This compared well with the updated annual costs of closure or partial closure first considered in the 1964 report, the current estimates being:

(a) Closing the entire canal but retaining it in water   £42,820
(b) Closing the upper part of the canal from Double locks
    and retaining it in water   £28,470
(c) Closing the entire canal and draining it   £19,970
(d) Closing the upper part of the canal from Double locks
    and draining it   £24,095

The report recommended that the canal should continue to be operated as at present, but with increased finance for maintenance and repairs.

The second report, *The River Exe, Exeter Canal and lands adjoining,* had also been produced by the city engineer & surveyor and town clerk, aided on this occasion by the city planning officer. It was an outline plan to conserve the existing facilities and to increase opportunities for the enjoyment of the area by the public. Schemes proposed included picnic areas, a bird sanctuary, and a bible garden. No costs were given, nor detailed plans prepared, as consultations would be needed to assess the demand. Once again the city council deferred making an immediate decision on the future of the canal and the additional finance required

1. *The Prospect of the Custom House from Trew's Ware c.*1743. Note the sailing ship about to enter the canal from Exeter quay.

2.   Opening ceremony at Exeter canal basin, 1830.

3. Ships at Exeter quay, 1896.
4. (*opposite page*) The Hudson's Bay Company ketch *Nonsuch* at Exeter canal basin, 1969.

5. Exeter canal basin and quay, 1969.

6. Ships at King's Arms sluice, 1896.

7. Remains of Exeter & Crediton Navigation lock at Exe Bridge North, 1973.

8. Countess Wear swing-bridges, 1979.

9. Repairs at Double locks, *c.*1920.

10. Topsham lock entrance, 1972.

11. The Holman family fleet, 1858.

12.   Annual inspection cruise at Turf, 1886.

13.   Turf lock from the air, 1982.

14. National Benzole tanker
Ben Johnson near Exeter, 1958.

15. Sludge vessel *Countess Wear*, now the only commercial user of the canal, 1979.

for maintenance and repairs. In May 1970 there was another change in the administration of the waterway, which now passed to the new arts and recreation committee (later to be known as the leisure committee).

The 1969 report did not specifically mention the state of the canal buildings, though they were often in disrepair. The swing-bridge cottage at Countess Wear was vandalised soon after it was vacated and was demolished by the early 1970s. The sluice-keeper's cottage at King's Arms sluice was demolished by accident, the contractor having mistaken this 'cottage by a swing-bridge' for the swing-bridge cottage at Countess Wear! Earlier, *Double Locks Hotel* had been threatened. Fortunately, I.S.C.A. intervened and took over the tenancy of the 18th-century hotel (in reality an inn). I.S.C.A., the Roman name for Exeter, also forms the initial letters of the International Sailing Craft Association, the registered charity that runs the maritime museum.[12]

One improvement for road traffic on the Exeter by-pass was the construction of a second bridge across the canal at Countess Wear. The new bridge, of the lifting type normally seen on the Llangollen branch of the Shropshire Union Canal and on the Brecon and Abergavenny Canal, was ready for use by summer 1972. An elevated control cabin was built above the older swing-bridge to give a better view for controlling traffic.[13]

Soon after the maritime museum opened two unusual craft sailed up the canal. One was a replica of the Hudson's Bay Company's first ship, the 50-ton ketch *Nonsuch,* built at Appledore, North Devon, for the company's 300th anniversary celebrations. She arrived at Turf on 15 August 1969, on the start of a five-day visit to Exeter. Later, the three-masted schooner *Charlotte Rhodes* came up to the quay on several occasions in 1971 for the filming of the B.B.C. television series *The Onedin Line.* Much of the filming for the early episodes of this serial was carried out at the quay and in the Exe estuary, as was a second series in 1976.[14]

A new acquisition for the maritime museum, the 40-ton Bridgwater Dock steam dredger *Bertha,* arrived in November 1971. Given by British Rail, and built by Brunel in 1844, she arrived just six months too late for the city council. They had had to pay £2,000 for dredging the gut by the quay to allow *The Onedin Line* filming to take place. Commercial traffic had continued to fall to 852 tons in 1970 and 696 tons in 1971. The last regular trader was the petroleum tanker *Esso Jersey,* the Dutch coaster *Jenjo* making an occasional voyage up the canal with timber for Gabriel Wade & English Ltd.[15]

Commercial trade ceased in the early part of 1972 when the Esso Depot at Exeter was closed and the tanks dismantled, the *Esso Jersey* being switched to coastal work. In this year Devon County Council decided that study should be made of the recreational use and potential of the Exe Estuary. The Water Act of 1973 caused a change in ownership of the *SW2* which, from 1 April 1974, was transferred to the South West Water Authority and renamed *Countess Wear.*[16]

By 1974 the canal banks were leaking badly, but a recommendation by the city council's officers that £50,000 be spent on repairing the banks, locks and lock gates that year was turned down by the leisure committee on 1 July. Instead of the planned three-year improvement programme costing £90,000 they asked the resources and performance review sub-committee to halt maintenance work whilst a further investigation was carried out. This was to consider the possibility of closing the canal to commercial traffic, which now consisted of the *Countess Wear.* It was suggested that it might be possible to re-route the sewage from Countess Wear to Topsham. Claiming that the waterway was now costing the equivalent of £100,000 a year to run, one member suggested that it be filled in and a road built on its bed.[17]

The resources and performance review sub-committee met the following evening. The council's chief executive, Mr. P. McCarthy, told members that the city council had a legal duty to maintain the canal, and if it had to be closed through lack of maintenance the council might be involved in claims for damages. He said, 'My advice to you is that you have no choice—either you spend this money or gamble on nothing going wrong'. The sub-committee agreed to the expenditure and decided to investigate whether they could charge the South West Water Authority a fee for the use of the canal by the sludge vessel *Countess Wear.* Claims were made at the meeting that she was sailing up and down too fast, causing damage to the banks.[18]

On and after 18 August 1975 headroom below the M5 viaduct was limited to 33 feet, though this increased to 36 feet when it was completed. One of the last ships to visit the city basin before the height restrictions came into force was training ship *Royalist.* It was to be her last visit as the masts were too tall to pass under the motorway. A de-masting crane was provided at Turf lock for yachts cruising to the city basin.[19]

Devon County Council's *Exe Estuary Study* was published in July 1975. Perhaps its most important recommendation was that the 10 authorities responsible for the estuary and its shore should meet on a regular basis to co-ordinate their duties and obligations. Dealing with the Exeter Canal, the study noted:

> The potential of the canal as a country park was recognised by the former Exeter City Council in a report *The River Exe, Exeter Canal and lands adjoining.* It suggested that fishing and boating should be encouraged and car parks and picnic sites provided, and access from the upper river to the estuary would be retained. A detailed assessment of these proposals is now being undertaken.

Topsham lock was taken out of use in spring 1976 because the gates were unsafe, the entrance from the canal being stanked off with steel sheet piling. The 1829 Exeter Canal Act, which amongst other provisions had sanctioned the building of Topsham lock, specifically noted it 'shall at all Times for ever hereafter be maintained and kept in good Repair and Condition'. Though there may be justifiable economic reasons for not making the necessary repairs, it is possible that the city council may be in breach of this Act of Parliament for failure to do so.

From 1 May 1976 pleasure craft charges were increased to £39 for a weekend return trip along the canal, these covering the overtime costs of operating Countess Wear swing-bridge and the locks. From 1 April 1978 these charges

EXETER CITY COUNCIL

SCHEDULE OF CONDITIONS, DUES AND CHARGES

FOR COMMERCIAL VESSELS, PLEASURE CRAFT AND YACHTS

USING THE PORT OF EXETER INCLUDING THE EXETER SHIP CANAL

APPLICABLE ON AND FROM 1ST APRIL 1978

EXETER SHIP CANAL

2. LOCKING ALL VESSELS

   Price of locking through one or more Locks (one direction only):-

Rowing boats	£1.70p
Other vessels	£5.00p

   Subject to a 25% discount where two or more vessels use the facilities offered by the City Council at any one time.

3. ASSISTANCE (COMPULSORY) FOR ALL VESSELS USING CANAL

   Price per passage one way:-

   (a) On week-days other than Saturdays or Bank Holidays £6.00p

   (b) On Saturdays, Sundays and Bank Holidays £17.00p

   Subject to a 25% discount where two or more vessels use the facilities offered by the City Council at any one time.

4. COMMERCIAL VESSELS

   Price per passage one way, in addition to the due under 5:-

   (a) For each passage during the hours of darkness on a week-day and during daylight hours on Saturdays, Sundays and Bank Holidays. £25.00p

   (b) For each passage during the hours of darkness on Saturdays, Sundays and Bank Holidays. £35.00p

   NOTE: "Hours of Darkness" means the hours between one hour after sunset and one hour before sunrise and "Daylight Hours" means such hours as are not "Hours of Darkness".

5. WEEK-END WORKING - ALL VESSELS TRAVERSING THE CANAL ON SATURDAYS AND SUNDAYS

   Additional Charge per one way passage. £17.00p

Figure 15.

were doubled (*see* page 85), and at the time of writing, April 1984, the charge
is £112.70. Following numerous protests by boat owners, the chief engineer,
Mr. Donald Sture, was asked in May 1978 what effect the increased charges
had on weekend users. He gave the simple answer, 'We never have any'. The high
charges were also blamed for the termination of the passenger boat service from
the city basin to Turf which had begun in 1976.[20]

Earlier, at the end of the 1977 season, the canal had to be closed from
24 September for repairs to Turf lock. A casting holding the bottom of one
of the 18-ton outer gates had fractured in three places and the heel post, the
vertical beam on which the gate swivels, also had to be renewed. A dam was
built to hold back the water while the lock was drained and the repairs made.[21]

In October 1977 I.S.C.A. made a tentative approach to the Dartington Amenities Research Trust about a study of the canal, basin and quay. The object was to
see if more could be done to improve the environment and the earning capacity
of the maritime museum and canal. Though the city council were unable to
join in the proposed study, in the early part of 1978 they called in R.P.A.
Management, a London firm of consultants, to prepare a comprehensive development plan for the canal which would attract investment to:

1. Eliminate the current operating deficit.
2. Enhance the standing of Exeter as the Regional Capital of the South
   West.
3. Attract more visitors to the City and its environs.
4. Fully develop the potential of a presently under-utilised resource.
5. Provide the residents of Exeter with additional amenities.

The report was published in November 1978. In comments on the state of the
canal it noted that, apart from a few parts protected with steel sheet piling, the
banks were crumbling or overgrown, and in some cases were a safety hazard. Of
the two remaining locks (Topsham having been closed), both had antiquated
gates and operating mechanism. Fortunately the staff had the necessary skills
to pass craft on passage through the locks. At Countess Wear the traffic flow was
about 18,000 vehicles a day and serious disruption to this traffic would be caused
when the bridges were opened for canal craft. The current cost of maintenance
was estimated at £70,000 per annum, to which had to be added an additional
£90,000 spent on major works such as lock gates in 1977–78. It was considered
that a similar sum would be incurred on repairs in the current year.

Four initial recommendations were made in the R.P.A. Management Report
Exeter Canal and River Developments. These can be summarised as:

(a) *New Industries*. To encourage a developer to bring new industries
     and jobs, such as boat-building and sales, to the city basin and
     canal. If the development were large enough it would warrant
     essential repair work to the canal banks and the modernisation
     of the locks, improve access and promote Exeter as a centre for
     inland and off-shore boating.

(b) *Holidays.* To provide a caravan park for touring caravans adjacent
to the canal and a complex of houseboats for holiday letting
on the canal, and for the development of *Double Locks Hotel.*

(c) *Visitors.* To build on the excellent start made by the maritime
museum by taking a more direct involvement in the financing,
planning and running of that facility, and for the redevelopment
of sheds and buildings on the quay to house other collections.

(d) *Marina.* To begin a 'ribbon development' marina, starting at Turf
lock basin by providing safe canal moorings at attractive rates.

The consultants admitted 'There is, in effect, no completely right answer for the
total area but a start should be made with the above scheme quickly'.

The report was considered by the city council's policy committee (who had
commissioned it) on 28 November. The suggestion for a marina, caravan park,
boatyard, etc., met with immediate objections, only one member speaking in
their favour. The opposition can best be summed up in the comments of
Mr. Howard Marsh, who said, 'If you ask me whether I would like to destroy the
natural beauty of the area to save the ratepayers £70,000 a year, the answer
is "No".' However, the committee agreed to receive the report, circulate copies
to all interested parties and also hold discussions with I.S.C.A.[22]

There was a more immediate problem to consider—the state of the *Turf Hotel.*
A survey in autumn 1978 had shown that there were several defects in the
building. Temporary repairs were authorised and the management sub-committee
called for a report on the future of the hotel and the operation of the lock. A
structural survey showed that repairs would exceed £70,000, though if part of
the building were to be demolished and the other made safe the cost would be
between £30,000 and £35,000. It was decided to ask for tenders for demolition.
News of this decision reached I.S.C.A. at the end of March 1979. They had
previously made a number of approaches to obtain the building and, when a
plea for a stay of demolition failed, they applied to the Department of the
Environment to have the building listed. The D.o.E. agreed to list the hotel as
being of historic interest, effectively putting paid to any immediate prospects
of demolition.

The city council then advertised for offers for a 99-year lease of *Turf Hotel*
and, to safeguard their position, also applied for listed building consent to
demolish the hotel on the grounds that it was dangerous. I.S.C.A. was one of
eight applicants for the lease, considering the control of the *Turf Hotel* as vital
to the future of the maritime museum. They had received advice that they should
extend their interests to cover the whole canal and saw this interest working in
some form of partnership with the city council.

I.S.C.A. suggested a price agreed between valuers for the hotel, though they
took the view that the high cost of repairs meant its present value to the city
council was nil. On 19 June it was resolved that the lease of the *Turf Hotel*
be given to two other applicants who had offered a premium of £20,000.
I.S.C.A. then made an offer of a similar amount and a special meeting of the
policy committee was held on 13 July to consider this new move. Though there

was opposition to the tenancy being granted to I.S.C.A., an extraordinary meeting of the city council approved this change of plan by one vote on 24 July.[23]

Why had there been a change of attitude by the city council? I.S.C.A. had long wished for the redevelopment of the basin, to make Exeter a real attraction for the growing number of boat-owners. Plans to this effect were briefly discussed in a local newspaper in January 1971, though they remained a dream because of the financial climate at that time. In its first decade of operation the maritime museum had grown from strength to strength and by 1979 its income had grown to £80,000, and 10 paid staff were employed. I.S.C.A. was now using warehouses at the city basin and at the quay, housing static exhibits, whilst the wharfinger's office had become their headquarters. *Double Locks Hotel* had been saved from demolition when they took over the tenancy and now a similar situation would occur with the *Turf Hotel.* The small wire-guided ferry that connected the quay with the city basin had also been saved from closure by I.S.C.A.[24]

At about the time the R.P.A. Management report on the development of the canal was published, I.S.C.A. was making its own approaches to the city council. They wanted a 99-year lease of the quay and most of the city basin, and to develop these areas according to plans to be agreed. Simultaneously I.S.C.A. contacted the fund-raising Wells Associates organisation to discuss ways of raising the money for the 99-year lease. These discussions grew into the idea of including the entire canal and all relevant buildings, such as the quay and city basin, in one large trust. This would be established by the city council and I.S.C.A., with the aim or preserving the canal and port of Exeter and to control the development of the area.[25]

In June 1979 the press reported:

> A major deal to expand Exeter Maritime Museum and improve the quay and basin area may be struck between the council and the museum.
>
> If the deal goes through the International Sailing Craft Association, which runs the museum, would lease the council-owned property in the historic basin and quay areas.
>
> It would pay a single premium at full market value of about £1 million.
>
> In return the council would use the money to offset canal losses and pay for maintenance and modernisation.
>
> The I.S.C.A. want to carry out a development scheme over 15 years.
>
> It includes a tea room and restaurant, development of quay sheds and cellars, to house museum craft and workshops, new toilets, accommodation for a caretaker and rationalisation of trading on the quay.
>
> Another idea is to use the customs house as a museum on the commercial history of Exeter.
>
> A working party is due to study how cash for the proposals deal could be raised.[26]

The R.P.A. Management report on the development of the canal had now been overtaken by subsequent events. On 8 January 1980 the joint policy and leisure committees decided to abandon the idea of a marina at the *Turf Hotel* because of the objections. The possible development of caravans, houseboats and *Double Locks Hotel* was deferred for six months 'because of other decisions involving the canal'. It was the death knell of that report as, on 15 July, the city council accepted and approved the Wells Associates report on the formation of an Exeter Canal and Quay Trust. I.S.C.A. had already accepted and approved this on 5 June.[27]

The city council agreed on 31 July that two charitable trusts be set up. The first, an operating company, would promote and control the various aims envisaged in improving the quay, museum and canal. This would have a committee of 15, who would elect a chairman from amongst their number, being composed of:

      8 from Exeter City Council
      3 from the Maritime Museum
      1 from Devon County Council
      1 from the South-west Tourist Board
      2 Independent.

The second charitable trust would be a development trust, having four trustees who would raise and control the funds to finance the operating company. The city council also agreed to advance £38,000 to the operating company during the first 18 months. Wells Associates were appointed 'to get the fund raising off the ground'. The cost of restoring buildings and carrying out essential repair work on the canal was estimated to be £645,500.[28]

One problem to resolve was that of rents, as the city council wanted the maritime museum to pay the current economic rate for premises previously occupied rent free. In fairness, the maritime museum was already contributing nearly £4,000 in rent and a similar sum in rates for premises occupied on the quay. Furthermore, the only museum that paid a rental in excess of £1,000 per annum was the Museum of Modern Art at Oxford, and this was offset by a larger grant from the Arts Council. Though a rental valuation of £21,250 per annum was agreed between the respective valuers it was obvious that the additional charge could not be met from income. Consequently the city council made a grant of £14,500 for the year 1981, receiving this back as rent![29]

Turf lock was closed from 18 June to 18 September 1981 whilst repairs costing more than £160,000 were undertaken. These involved building a coffer dam at the lock tail, before stabilising the outer pier heads which were unsafe. Each carried a 15-ton lock gate. Repairs were also made to the lock gates and stonework. Then the coffer dam was cut off below the water level and left to act as an additional support for the entrance walls.[30]

Turf lock was also in the news in 1982, with the purchase of the *Water Mongoose,* a 47-ft. passenger launch seating fifty-six. An ex-British Waterways vessel, she was previously used on the Regent's Canal for trips to London Zoo. Her new duties include passenger trips from Countess Wear to Turf, a very popular facility which has created much new business at the hotel.[31]

A solution to the worrying problem of the maritime museum rent was proposed by the Development Trust. It would seek a 99-year lease from the city council on all the property in which it had an interest at the quay, the city basin and the canal and then raise the money to buy the lease. Legal matters move very slowly and it was not until 3 February 1983 that the lease was signed, the premium being £150,000, of which £130,000 was provided by the National Heritage Fund.[32]

Is this the start of a brighter future for the Exeter Canal? It is, at least, working towards the conclusion of the now-forgotten R.P.A. Management report:

> . . . every effort should be made to retain the canal and other facilities, if possible in full working order to preserve its original purpose, if for no other reason than it is impossible to determine the needs of future generations of Exonians who may feel betrayed if irreplaceable assets were thrown away because they have no obvious use for a period in their history.

NOTES

ABBREVIATIONS

C.A.B.   Chamber Act Book
D.R.O.   Devon Record Office
E.C.C.   Exeter City Council
N.C.M.   Navigation Committee Minutes

Chapter One (pages 1 to 9)

1. For further details of this and later inquisitions and for the early history of the River Exe, *see* E. A. G. Clark, *The Ports of the Exe Estuary 1660–1860*, 1968, and his University of London Ph.D. thesis *The Estuarine Ports of the Exe and Teign, with special reference to the period 1660–1860: A Study in Historical Geography*, 1956 (D.R.O.); also P. C. de la Garde's article 'On the Antiquity and invention of the Lock Canal of Exeter' in *Archaeologia*, vol. XXVIII, 1838.

2. P. C. de la Garde, *Archaeologia*, op. cit.

3. E. A. G. Clark, *The Ports of the Exe Estuary*, op. cit., p. 22. A. M. Jackson, in his article 'Medieval Exeter, the Exe and the Earldom of Exeter' in *Reports and Transactions of the Devonshire Association*, vol. 104, 1972, pp. 57–79, considers that the river was blocked by Baldwin de Redvers, sixth Earl of Devon, between 1239–45 and that the weir was broken down in 1263. The barrier was re-erected 'well before 1290'.

4. Quoted by P. C. de la Garde, *Archaeologia*, op. cit.

5. John Hooker, *The Description of the Citie of Excester*, ed. by W. J. Harte, J. W. Schopp and H. Tapley Soper, 1919–47.

6. *Powderham Castle*, official guide book, 1972, p. 32. Obstruction to Shipping on the Exe, *c.* 1461 (D.R.O.), Misc. Roll 3 m. 7.

7. Quoted by P. C. de la Garde, *Archaeologia*, op. cit. 31 Henry VIII, c.4.

8. C.A.B., 23 March 1543.

9. P. C. de la Garde, *Archaeologia*, op. cit.

10. C.A.B., 27 October 1560.

11. P. C. de la Garde, *Archaeologia*, op. cit.

12. C.A.B., 15 December 1563.

13. This description and much of the history of the Lighter Canal is based on W. B. Stephens' article, 'The Exeter Lighter Canal 1566–1698' in the *Journal of Transport History*, May 1957.

14. Bodleian Library, Oxford, Twynne-Langbaine MS. 1, f. 76. I am grateful to Professor A. W. Skempton, Imperial College, London, for this information.

15. P. C. de la Garde, *Archaeologia*, op. cit.

16. C.A.B., 30 July 1567.

17. Ibid., April 1573. P. C. de la Garde, *Archaeologia*, op. cit.

18. C.A.B., 4 June 1579. E. A. G. Clark, *The Ports of the Exe Estuary*, op. cit., p. 31.

19. C.A.B., 13 March 1619, 12 August 1630 and 3 November 1631.

20. Ibid., 4 March 1634.

21. Noted on the fly-leaf of the parish register of St Sidwell, Exeter.

22. C.A.B., February 1675.

23. W. B. Stephens, *Seventeenth Century Exeter: A Study of Industrial and Commercial Development, 1625–1688*, 1958, pp. 103-5.

24. C.A.B., 23 June 1696.

25. *Journeys of Celia Fiennes,* ed. C. Morris, 1947.

Chapter Two (pages 11 to 19)

1. *The Chamber and William Bayley,* 1698 (D.R.O.).

2. C.A.B., May 1699.

3. For a full account of the woollen trade, *see* E. A. G. Clark, *The Ports of the Exe Estuary,* op. cit.

4. C.A.B., June 1699. 'Chapple's Manuscript Occurrence under the year 1699', quoted in the *Devon and Exeter Gazette,* 17 December 1928.

5. *Case of the Mayor and Chamber of Exeter against the Bill for making a Navigable Canal from Taunton to Topsham,* February 1796 (D.R.O.).

6. C.A.B., July 1700 and January 1701.

7. Ibid., October 1704, March 1709 and July 1726.

8. E. A. G. Clark, *The Ports of the Exe Estuary,* op. cit., pp. 206 and 223.

9. C.A.B., April 1729

10. E. A. G. Clark, *The Ports of the Exe Estuary,* op. cit., p. 223. *Western Morning News,* 1 August 1971.

11. Charles Hadfield, *The Canals of South West England,* 1967, p. 37.

12. *Case . . . against the Bill for making a Navigable Canal from Taunton to Topsham,* op. cit.

13. E. A. G. Clark, *The Ports of the Exe Estuary,* op. cit., pp. 118–23.

14. *Exeter Flying Post,* 11 October 1792.

15. Ibid., 1 November 1792.

16. For further details of the Bristol & Western and Taunton & Uphill canals *see* Charles Hadfield, *The Canals of South West England,* op. cit., pp. 332–36.

17. *Exeter Flying Post,* 11 July and 13 August 1793. For the biography of William Jessop *see* Charles Hadfield and A. W. Skempton, *William Jessop, Engineer,* 1979.

18. *Mr. Jessop's Report on his survey of The Grand Western Canal,* November 1793 (D.R.O.).

19. *Exeter Flying Post,* 16 July 1795.

20. *Case . . . against the Bill for making a Navigable Canal from Taunton to Topsham,* op. cit.

21. 36 Geo. III, c.46, 24 March 1796.

22. Letter to Richard Hall Clark, Esq., from Sir George Yonge, Bt., dated 26 April 1810 (Somerset Record Office).

23. *An Authentic Description of the Kennet and Avon Canal,* 1810 (reprinted by the Kennet and Avon Canal Trust, 1969).

24. For the full history of the Grand Western Canal *see* Helen Harris, *The Grand Western Canal,* 1973.

25. *Woolmer's Exeter and Plymouth Gazette,* 2 October 1830.

26. Noted on the title page of the navigation committee's first minute book.

Chapter Three (pages 21 to 32)

1. *Exeter Flying Post,* 22 November 1792 and 24 January 1793.

2. *Canal from Topsham to Exeter, Crediton, etc.,* 24 January 1793 (D.R.O.).

3. MS. *Mr. Houghton: Answer and Observations,* January 1793 in Calmady Hamlyn of Leawood papers (D.R.O.).

4. *Exeter Flying Post,* 7 February 1793.

5. Ibid.

6. Ibid. and 14 February 1793.

7. MS. Address by Christopher Hamlyn to the Public Devonshire Canal subscribers (21 February 1793?) in Calmady Hamlyn of Leawood papers (D.R.O.).

8. *Exeter Flying Post*, 28 February 1793.

9. Ibid., 21 February and 21 March 1793.

10. For further details of the Tamar Manure Navigation and Tavistock Canal *see* Charles Hadfield, *The Canals of South West England*, op. cit., pp. 124-35, and Carolyn Hedges, *The Tavistock Canal*, 1975.

11. *Exeter Flying Post*, 28 March, 16 May and 29 August 1793. *Sherborne Mercury*, 1 July and 14 October 1793.

12. Deposited plan, 1793 (D.R.O.).

13. *A Report by the Committee of the intended Public Devonshire Canal*, 17 October 1793 (D.R.O.). *Exeter Flying Post*, 24 October 1793.

14. MS. *Letter to Members and Answers*, by Christopher Hamlyn (17 October 1793?) in Calmady Hamlyn of Leawood papers (D.R.O.).

15. *Exeter Flying Post*, 14 November 1793.

16. Ibid., 5 December 1793.

17. Ibid. For the history of Bude Canal *see* Helen Harris and Monica Ellis, *The Bude Canal*, 1972.

18. Ibid., 17 April 1794.

19. For further details of the Torrington or Rolle Canal *see* Charles Hadfield, *The Canals of South West England*, op. cit., pp. 135-41.

20. MS. *Remarks on the report of Mr. Whitworth and Messrs. Bolton and Bentley as delivered to the Committee of the Public Devonshire Canal, Crediton, Febry 11th, 1794*, and MS. Letter from Robert Whitworth, n.d., both in Calmady Hamlyn of Leawood papers (D.R.O.).

21. *Exeter Flying Post*, 20 February 1794.

22. Ibid., 1 January 1795.

23. Ibid., 23 October 1800.

24. Ibid., 17 June 1824.

25. 41 Geo. III, c.61.

26. *Exeter Flying Post*, 22 September 1808. Charles Vancouver, *General View of the Agriculture of the County of Devon*, 1808, p. 379.

27. *Exeter Flying Post*, 3 August 1809, 13 June to 22 August 1811 and 2 July 1812. T. Moore, *History of Devonshire*, 1829-36, p. 73. Letter from Exeter & Crediton Navigation clerk dated 24 September 1818 in Papers of the Navigation Committee, 1815-29 (D.R.O.).

28. *Waterways News*, March 1978, p. 4.

Chapter Four (pages 33 to 43)

1. James Green's article 'Continuation of the Memoir of the Canal of Exeter, from 1819 to 1830' in *Minutes of Proceedings of the Institution of Civil Engineers, Vol. IV, Session 1845*.

2. N.C.M., 18 December 1820.

3. Ibid., 5 February 1822.

4. The trade of Exeter is covered in detail in E. A. G. Clark's *The Ports of the Exe Estuary*, op. cit.

5. James Green, *Minutes... of the Institution of Civil Engineers, 1845*, op. cit.

6. N.C.M., 7 June 1824.

7. James Green, *Minutes... of the Institution of Civil Engineers, 1845*, op. cit.

8. N.C.M., 4 August 1824. *Report of the Committee appointed to examine the Expenditure on the Canal*, 1836 (D.R.O.).

9. N.C.M., 7 and 28 December 1824, 18 and 31 January, 18 April and 1 June 1825.

10. Ibid., 3 August and 2 November 1825.

11. James Green, *Minutes... of the Institution of Civil Engineers, 1845*, op. cit.

12 Ibid.

13. *Report of . . . the Expenditure on the Canal*, op. cit.

14. James Green, *Minutes . . . of the Institution of Civil Engineers, 1845*, op. cit.

15. *Exeter Flying Post*, 20 September 1827.

16. Ibid.

17. N.C.M., 5 December 1827. Law papers: Attorney General and Mayor of Exeter v. Davy, 1827 (D.R.O.). *Woolmer's Exeter and Plymouth Gazette*, 4-11 June 1827. Clive N. Ponsford, *Topsham and the Exe Estuary*, 1979, pp. 23-26.

18. *Report of . . . the Expenditure on the Canal*, op. cit.

19. *Exeter Flying Post*, 18 December 1828. N.C.M., 1 January 1829.

20. 10 Geo. IV, c.47.

21. Report of the Town Clerk re Canal Mortgages, 12 July 1880 (D.R.O.).

22. N.C.M., 7 October 1829. Law papers: Attorney General . . . v. Davy, op. cit.

23. *Woolmer's Exeter and Plymouth Gazette*, 15-20 September 1830. N.C.M., 28 September 1830.

24. *Woolmer's Exeter and Plymouth Gazette*, 2 October 1830.

25. Ibid.

Chapter Five (pages 45 to 56)

1. Quoted by Charles Hadfield, *The Canals of South West England*, op. cit., p. 23.

2. D. M. Bradbeer, *The Story of the Manor and Port of Topsham*, 1968, pp. 30-31.

3. N.C.M., 7 March 1832

4. Ibid., 11 February and 4 March 1834.

5. *Report of . . . the Expenditure on the Canal*, op. cit.

6. *Proceedings of the Municipal Corporations Commission of Exeter taken by Thomas Latimer*, 1833, 5th day, p. 55.

7. *Report of . . . the Expenditure on the Canal*, op. cit.

8. *Exeter Canal: Account of Extra Works and Sums Expended which were not included in the estimates*, statement by James Green dated 5 April 1837 (D.R.O.).

9. *Minutes of a meeting of the late Chamber of the City of Exeter summoned at the request of the present Council to report on the statement made by James Green on 5 April 1837*, 19 August 1837 (D.R.O.).

10. N.C.M., 6 July 1837, 2 August 1838, 3 December 1840, 15 February and 5 April 1841.

11. Ibid., 2 September 1841.

12. Ibid., 26 September 1840, 1 April and 7 October 1841, 1 September and 1 December 1842, 2 February 1843.

13. 3 and 4 Vic., c.74.

14. N.C.M., 7 March 1843. James Cossins, *Reminiscences of Exeter Fifty Years Since*, 2nd edn., 1878, p. 54.

15. N.C.M., 19 September 1843.

16. Report of the Town Clerk re Canal Mortgages, 12 July 1880 (D.R.O.).

17. Letter from G. Stabback dated 26 February 1846 in Papers relating to the Canal Mortgages (D.R.O.).

18. *Minutes of the General Committee of the Council and Canal Creditors, 24 March 1846* in Canal Mortgage papers, op. cit.

19. *Report of the Special Finance Committee of the Council, 9 December 1846* in Canal Mortgage papers, op. cit. Robert Newton, *Victorian Exeter*, 1968, p. 46. *Exeter Flying Post*, 23 April 1846.

20. For the railway history of the area *see* E. T. McDermot, (rev. C. R. Clinker), *History of the Great Western Railway*, 1964; R. H. Gregory, *The South Devon Railway*, 1982; C. G. Maggs, *Railways to Exmouth*, 1980; C. F. Dendy Marshall, *A History of the Southern Railway*, 1962; and David St John Thomas, *A Regional History of the Railways of Great Britain: Vol. I The West Country*, 4th edn., 1973.

21. N.C.M., 4 October 1849.

22. Ibid., 15 April, 6 July and 3 August 1848. *Woolmer's Exeter and Plymouth Gazette,* 22 January 1848.

23. N.C.M., 7 December 1848 and 1 August 1850. G. Halford Thompson, *The Exeter Canal: How to restore its Trade,* 1876 (D.R.O.).

24. N.C.M., 6 June and 1 August 1850.

25. Ibid., 2 July 1851, 4 March 1852 and 5 January 1854.

26. Report of the Town Clerk re Canal Mortgages, 12 July 1880 (D.R.O.). Canal Suit: Terms of Settlement, 6 September 1860 (D.R.O.).

27. N.C.M., 5 January and 2 February 1854, 4 November 1856, 1 January and 2 February 1857.

Chapter Six (pages 57 to 67)

1. For further details of the Holman family and their fleet *see* D. M. Bradbeer, *The Story of the Manor and Port of Topsham,* op. cit., and the article by W. M. Benn, 'The Exe has proud history of shipbuilding' in *Express and Echo,* 11 August 1967; also Clive N. Ponsford, *Topsham and the Exe Estuary,* 1979, pp. 28-32.

2. G. Oliver, *History of the City of Exeter,* 1861.

3. E. A. G. Clark, *The Estuarine Ports of the Exe and Teign,* op. cit. pp. 631-32. N.C.M., 6 May 1871 and 10 October 1876.

4. Special Canal Committee in conference with shippers, etc., 2 and 3 February 1866 in Miscellaneous Reports and other papers connected with the Canal, 1864-80 (D.R.O.).

5. N.C.M., 11 May 1868.

6. Ibid., 5 March 1863 and 8 June 1867.

7. Ibid., 4 and 17 July 1867.

8. William Beardmore's Report dated 20 September 1867 in Miscellaneous Reports and other papers . . ., op. cit.

9. Minute Book of the Canal Creditors, 4 December 1867 (D.R.O.).

10. *Case submitted to Mr. Bagshawe, Q.C., and his Opinion thereon,* 15 November 1880 (D.R.O.).

11. N.C.M., 27 July 1868 and 25 February 1869. William Beardmore's Report dated 5 August 1868 in Miscellaneous Reports and other papers . . ., op. cit.

12. N.C.M., 10 May 1870.

13. G. Halford Thompson, *The Exeter Canal: How to restore its Trade,* op. cit. Report of the Town Clerk re Canal Mortgages, op. cit.

14. G. Halford Thompson, *The Exeter Canal: How to restore its Trade,* op. cit.

15. N.C.M., 10 October 1876 and 5 January 1880. *Woolmer's Exeter and Plymouth Gazette,* 22-27 September 1880.

16. Report of the Town Clerk re Canal Mortgages, op. cit.

17. Ibid.

18. Ibid. Robert Newton, *Victorian Exeter,* op. cit., p. 208.

19. *Proposed terms of Settlement with the Canal Statutory Mortgages,* 1882 (D.R.O.).

20. 46 and 47 Vic., c.33.

Chapter Seven (pages 69 to 78)

1. E. A. G. Clark, *The Ports of the Exe Estuary,* op. cit., p. 222.

2. N.C.M., 4 March 1884.

3. Ibid., 29 July 1884, 11 January 1886, 4 January and 4 October 1887.

4. E. A. G. Clark, *The Estuarine Ports of the Exe and Teign,* op. cit., p. 73.

5. Ibid., pp. 177-78. N.C.M., 6 February 1894.

6. Canal Returns, 1888 and 1898.

7. N.C.M., 11 September 1894.

8. Ibid., 8 January, 7 August and 8 October 1895.

9. Ibid., 30 November 1897 and 2 June 1908.

10. Ibid., 23 September 1908.

11. Ibid., 1 March 1910.

12. Charles Hadfield, *The Canals of South West England*, op. cit., p. 25. *Annual Report of the City Engineer and Surveyor's Department*, 1911. N.C.M., 28 March 1911.

13. Ibid., 17 May 1915 and 22 May 1916.

14. Ibid., 8 February 1921 and 7 July 1922.

15. *Western Morning News*, 28 May 1924.

16. N.C.M., 17 June and 30 September 1924 and 10 February, 4 May and 17 November 1925.

17. Ibid., 14 February 1928 and 31 December 1929.

18. *Express and Echo*, 16 February 1935. N.C.M., 15 June 1933.

19. Ibid., 21 November 1933 and 2 January 1934.

20. *Express and Echo*, 12 January 1935.

21. Ibid., 22 December 1934 and 20 February 1935.

22. Ibid., 24 October 1935. *Annual Report of the City Engineer*, op. cit., 1938.

23. Ibid., 30 November 1937. *Annual Report of the City Engineer*, op. cit., 1938.

24. Ibid., 1938. N.C.M., 15 November 1938.

25. *Express and Echo*, 28 May 1969 and 26 July 1971. MS. *Port of Exeter: Note on History of Canal*, by J. Brierley, City Engineer & Surveyor, n.d. (D.R.O.).

26. N.C.M., 7 October 1947 and 6 June 1948.

27. Ibid., 6 June and 8 November 1950.

28. Ibid., 27 November 1951.

29. *Annual Report of the City Engineer*, op. cit., 1951–54.

30. N.C.M., 3 November 1953.

31. Ibid., 2 September 1953.

32. *Port of Exeter: Note on History*, op. cit. N.C.M., 30 March 1954.

33. Ibid, 1 February 1955. *Western Morning News*, 24 September 1954.

34. *A further consideration of the future of the Exeter Canal*, November 1969 (D.R.O.). N.C.M., 31 January 1956. *The Syren and Shipping*, 4 July 1956.

35. *Annual Report of the City Engineer*, op. cit., 1959–62. N.C.M., 4 September 1956 and 28 November 1961.

36. *Annual Reports of the City Engineer*, op. cit. 1962–64. *A further consideration . . . of the Exeter Canal*, op. cit.

37. *Annual Report of the City Engineer*, op. cit., 1964. *Express and Echo*, 12 June 1965.

Chapter Eight (pages 79 to 90)

1. *A further consideration . . . of the Exeter Canal*, op. cit. *Western Morning News*, 11 December 1964.

2. *Daily Telegraph*, 25 November 1965.

3. *Express and Echo*, 23 April 1965.

4. Ibid., 14 October 1966. *Western Morning News*, 30 September 1966. *A further consideration . . . of the Exeter Canal*, op. cit.

5. *Express and Echo*, 6 October 1966. *Western Morning News*, 30 September 1966.

6. Ibid., 30 November 1966.

7. Ibid.

8. *Annual Report of the City Engineer*, op. cit., 1966. N.C.M., 10 March 1965. *Western Morning News*, 18 July 1966.

9. N.C.M., 29 November 1966. *Daily Telegraph*, 15 August 1968. *A further consideration . . . of the Exeter Canal*, op. cit.

10. Ibid. *Exeter Maritime Museum,* official guide book. *Daily Telegraph Magazine,* 25 July 1969.

11. *Exeter Maritime Museum,* official guide book.

12. *Express and Echo,* 8 January 1971. *Western Morning News,* 18 February 1969.

13. Ibid., 12 April 1972.

14. *Express and Echo,* 1 May 1971. *The Onedin Line in Exeter,* n.d. (*c.* 1976).

15. *Daily Telegraph,* 24 November 1971. *Express and Echo,* 29 January 1972.

16. *Waterways World,* Spring 1972, p. 41.

17. *Western Morning News,* 2 July 1974.

18. Ibid., 3 July 1974.

19. *Sou'wester,* Autumn 1975 and Spring 1976.

20. *Express and Echo,* 25 May 1978.

21. *Express and Echo,* 20 October 1977.

22. *Exeter Weekly News,* 1 December 1978.

23. E.C.C. policy committee minutes, 13 July 1979. *I.S.C.A. Newsletter,* 12 September 1979.

24. *Express and Echo,* 8 January 1971.

25. *I.S.C.A. Newsletter,* 12 September 1979.

26. *Western Morning News,* 15 June 1979.

27. Ibid., 9 January 1980. *I.S.C.A. Newsletter,* 10 October 1980. *Western Times,* 11 January 1980.

28. *Express and Echo,* 1 July 1980. *Exeter Weekly News,* 4 July 1980.

29. *I.S.C.A. Newsletter,* 10 October 1980, 16 October 1981, 3 March 1982.

30. *Express and Echo,* 27 July 1981. *I.S.C.A. Newsletter,* 16 October 1981.

31. *Waterways World,* August 1982. *Express and Echo,* 29 May 1982.

32. *I.S.C.A. Newsletter,* 16 October 1981, 3 March 1982, October 1982, March 1983, October 1983.

Figure 16.   Exeter Maritime Museum logo, depicting some of the exhibits.

APPENDIX A

WALKING THE WATERWAY

THE 5¼ MILES LENGTH of the canal makes a pleasant walk with plenty of things of interest to look at on the way. Care should be taken with timings, as the *Turf Hotel* closes at 2.30 p.m. after the lunch-time session, and it is a long way to any alternative place of refreshment. On the return journey a diversion to Topsham is possible. A rowing-boat ferry operates from Topsham lock across the Exe estuary in summer months, giving a chance to visit the historic port which, like Exeter, has now lost virtually all of its commercial shipping. It is still an interesting place to see and has a wealth of old houses in its narrow streets. There are frequent bus and train services back to Exeter, and on Monday, Wednesday and Saturday afternoons Topsham museum is open at 25 The Strand. The museum contains many relics of the Holman family, whose fleet sailed from the port during the 19th century.

A brief guide to some of the most interesting 'sights to see' from the canal and the quay is given below. National Grid references are included to aid their location.

At the *quay,* look out for the *Custom House* (SX 919921) which dates from 1681 and was originally colonnaded at the front. Across the road is the *Fishmarket,* now housing some of the maritime museum exhibits. To the east of the Custom House is the *Wharfinger's Office,* built in 1778 and used as an office by I.S.C.A., the charitable trust that runs the maritime museum. More exhibits are to be found in the five-storeyed white limestone *Warehouse* (SX 920921) of 1835, just beyond the *Prospect Inn.* There is another inn, the *Port Royal,* a little way past a second five-storeyed warehouse, the latter partly used for storage by the museum. Close by the warehouse, a small wire-guided ferry takes foot passengers across the river to the canal basin (SX 921918) and the main part of the maritime museum. Before leaving the quay, notice the bollards. These are reputed to have been cannons used at the Battle of Waterloo.

The canal basin is fenced off, the larger craft floating in its waters whilst the smaller ones are kept in the Victorian warehouse. The museum is well worth a visit, though allow about half a day to do justice to its exhibits. To the north of the basin was the terminal of the branch line railway (SX 920919). Until Exeter gas works were demolished in 1973 the branch line was busy with coal, but is now only occasionally used for shunting operations to and from King's Asphalt Ltd. siding.

A wide pathway runs between the river and the maritime museum and leads to two swing-bridges. One crosses the entrance to King's Arms sluice (SX 922917), whose flood-gates lead to the River Exe. The sluice-keeper's house has been demolished and the clearance gives a good view of Trew's weir, about 150 yards down the river. The other bridge crosses the cut leading to the basin, giving access to the right-hand towing path. A towing path runs on both sides of the canal to Turf, the right-hand one being the easiest for walking. On this bank, by the swing-bridge, is the canal maintenance yard and next to it is the *Welcome Inn*. Around the corner from the inn is the wharf once used by the timber boats for Gabriel Wade & English Ltd.

It is less than a mile from the city basin to Salmon Pool bridge (SX 927907), a modern steel swing-bridge. The busy railway line from Paddington and Bristol to Paignton and Plymouth runs close to the canal and never deviates far from it on the way to Turf. In another half a mile *Double Locks Hotel* (SX 933900) is reached. The inn was built in the early 18th century and retains its stabling. It stands at the southernmost end of Double locks (315ft. by 36ft.). A truck was used to carry rowing boats around the lock, and traces of the rails it ran on can be seen on the left-hand towpath.

In another three quarters of a mile are the two bridges which carry the dual carriageway Exeter by-pass across the canal at Countess Wear. The nearer one (SX 940894) is a modern version of the lifting bridges used on the Llangollen branch of the Shropshire Union and Brecon & Abergavenny canals and was built in 1972. The other is a swing-bridge which has been in service since 1937. The headroom of three feet above water level makes it all but impossible to follow the towpath at this point. Great care should be taken when crossing the by-pass as over 18,000 vehicles use it on an average day.

The canal now begins to run close to the Exe estuary and, on the right hand, by the Alphin Brook. Soon comes the start of the Countess Wear sewage works complex (SX 946892), the home 'port' of the sludge vessel *Countess Wear*. She is usually moored beyond the complex, close to the wide pool that conveniently acts as a winding point, and which was built as a transhipment basin for the 1676 ship canal. At the far end of the pool is the M5 motorway viaduct, where the canal narrows. Near the end of this narrow and straight stretch was Lower sluice, the entrance to the navigation from 1676 to 1827.

The port of Topsham can be seen across the estuary and, nearly four miles from the city basin, is Topsham lock (SX 961880). The lock (88ft. by 25ft.) is out of action and stanked off from the canal by steel sheet piling. A few yards further on is a wooden swing-bridge, giving access to the left bank and to a pathway to Topsham ferry. The waterway now hugs the Exe estuary, running for the final 1¼ miles in an almost straight line to Turf, whilst the railway takes a more inland course. This area is the haunt of sea-birds and other wildlife, and a pair of binoculars is a useful asset.

Soon the shape of *Turf Hotel* comes into view, then the long basin with its narrow 29-ft. opening, and finally Turf lock (SX 964860). The lock (122ft. by 29ft.) has a demasting crane, so that yachts may pass under the motorway viaduct. There are also traffic signals, to indicate when craft may enter from the estuary. The hotel was designed by James Green and has extensive outbuildings, some of which were used as stabling for the horses that towed the ships. Walk down, past the lock, to the granite quays jutting out into the entrance channel. They are overgrown through lack of use, for the only regular user is now the sludge vessel *Countess Wear*. At least the beer still comes by boat to the *Turf Hotel*!

APPENDIX B

TABLE OF DISTANCES

Head of canal basin, Exeter

$\frac{1}{8}$					Junction with King's Arms sluice
$1\frac{1}{2}$	$1\frac{3}{8}$				Double locks
$2\frac{1}{4}$	$2\frac{1}{8}$	$\frac{3}{4}$			Countess Wear swing-bridge
$3\frac{3}{4}$	$3\frac{5}{8}$	$2\frac{1}{4}$	$1\frac{1}{2}$		Topsham lock entrance
$5\frac{1}{4}$	$5\frac{1}{8}$	$3\frac{3}{4}$	3	$1\frac{1}{2}$	Turf lock

APPENDIX C

BYE–LAWS OF 1829

I.—No boat, barge, or other vessel, to lie or abide to moor and ballast, load and unload, within *three hundred yards* of the lowest tideway entrance, at the mouth of the said Canal, below a certain place called *Turf,* under the penalty of *ten pounds* for every offence, to be paid by the Master or other person having the direction of such vessel.

II.—No vessel to be permitted to enter the Canal without the Master, or person having the direction of every such vessel, first *truly* and *correctly* reporting to the Keeper of the entrance-lock the depth of water which his vessel draws, and ascertaining from the said Keeper that there will be sufficient depth of water on the lower sill of the entrance-lock, on the same or following tide, for such vessel to enter the lock, under the penalty of *ten pounds.* And every person having the direction or command of any vessel, who shall make a false statement of the draft of water thereof, shall forfeit and pay the sum of *ten pounds.*

III.—In case of there being more than one vessel, and those of different draft of water, about to enter the Canal, the Master or other person having the direction of such vessels, shall obey the directions of the Keeper of the entrance-lock, as to the order and time of their entrance, (which such Lock-keeper is required to regulate, so that a smaller vessel may not be retarded by a greater vessel) under the penalty of *five pounds.*

IV.—If any vessel shall enter, or attempt to enter, the lock or basin, at Turf, without having on board a proper and sufficient quantity of warping-lines or ropes, the Master, or other person having the command thereof, shall, for each and every offence, forfeit and pay the sum of *one pound.*

V.—Any vessel about leaving the Canal or Basin, whether loaded or unloaded, is not to interfere of impede the entrance of any other vessel into the said Canal or Basins, but is to wait in such place and in such manner as the Lock-keeper or other Superintendent of the Canal shall direct, so as such vessel may depart without retarding or occasioning inconvenience to those vessels which are inward bound; and the Master or other person having the command of any vessel acting contrary to this bye-law, to forfeit the sum of *two pounds.*

VI.—Immediately on entering the Canal-Basin all vessels are to have their anchors on board and run in their bowsprits or jib-booms, where the same can be done; and every square-rigged vessel is to *peak* her yards, and to get her sprit-sail yard fore and aft, and keep them so whilst she continues within the Canal or

102

Basins; and if any Master, Bargeman, Boatman, or other person or persons in charge of any such vessel shall neglect or refuse so to do, or to slack down or heave in any mooring-tope or line, when thereunto required by the Wharfinger, or Sluice-keeper, or any Superintendent of the Canal, he or they shall, for every such offence, forfeit and pay the sum of *one pound*.

VII.—The Master or person having the command of any vessel, barge, or boat, drawing less than eight feet of water, attempting to pass *outward* through the entrance-lock at Turf, excepting during the hours of between four o'clock in the morning and nine o'clock in the evening, from March 25th to September 29th, and seven o'clock in the morning, and five o'clock in the evening, from the 29th September to the 25th March, to forfeit the sum of *one pound*.

VIII.—Vessels passing each other on the Canal are to keep as close as they safely can do to the starboard side thereof; and in case of two vessels meeting in a part of the Canal where there shall not be room for them to pass each other, then the vessel which is either empty or outward-bound shall turn or go back to some convenient passing place, and wait there, in order that the vessel which is laden or inward bound may get past her, and the Master or Owner of any empty or outward bound vessel refusing so to turn or lie by as aforesaid, or otherwise acting contrary to this bye-law, to forfeit the sum of *ten shillings*.

IX.—In passing along the Canal, all Masters, Bargemen, Boatmen, and persons in charge of vessels are to be particularly careful to avoid striking or rubbing against the banks on either side thereof, or against the bridges, stop gates, locks, weirs, or other works. And in case it shall appear to the Wharfinger, Collector, Sluice-keeper, or any Superintendent of the said Canal, that in so passing along, or using the Canal, Basins, and other works, any vessel shall strike against the banks, bridges, or other works, so as to break down or in any way injure the same, the Master and Owner of every such vessel, in addition to being liable to repair and make good all such damage, shall forefeit and pay, for every such offence, the sum of *two pounds*.

X.—All vessels navigating the Canal, whether towed by horses or otherwise, shall have a sufficient number of men, with proper hawsers or lines, out on each side of the Canal, to guide and manage such vessels, under the penalty of *one pound*.

XI.—The crews of all vessels passing on or using the Canal are to assist the Lock and Bridge Keepers in opening and closing the bridges and locks; and every Master, Bargeman, Boatman, or person belonging to any such vessel refusing so to assist the Lock or Bridge Keeper, or leaving any such lock or bridge before it is effectually closed and secured, shall, for every such offence, forfeit and pay the sum of *one pound*.

XII.—The Master, Owner, Boatman or Bargeman of any vessel, whether accidentally or otherwise obstructing, delaying, or interrupting the passage of vessels into, out of, upon, or through the Canal, shall, for every such offence, forefeit and pay the sum of *ten shillings* for every hour such obstruction shall be continued after notice by the Wharfinger, Sluice-keeper or Superintendent of the Canal, given to remove the same, together with the costs of getting rid of such obstruction.

XIII.—If the Master, Owner, Bargeman, Boatman, or person in charge of any ship, vessel, boat, or barge, so obstructing the free entrance or departure of vessels, or their free passage along the Canal as aforesaid, shall omit or neglect immediately to remove such obstruction, then the Wharfinger, Collector, Sluice-keeper, or any Superintendent of the Canal is to cause the same to be removed without delay, and to unload such vessel if necessary.

XIV.—If any person or persons shall, by any means, obstruct or cause to be obstructed, the way or passage over the bridge, towing-path, road, or wharf belonging to the Canal, and not immediately remove the same on notice given, such person or persons so offending, shall forfeit and pay the sum of *ten shillings* for every hour the same shall thereafter continue.

XV.—No vessel shall be allowed to moor in any part of the Canal but to such mooring posts as are placed for the purpose on the banks thereof, and then only by permission of the Wharfinger, Collector, or Superintendent of the Canal, under the penalty of *five pounds*.

XVI.—No vessel shall be allowed to remain moored in any part of the Canal without having at all times, whether by night or day, a sufficient number of proper persons on board thereof to take charge of the same, under the penalty of *five pounds* over and above the payment of all loss or damage either to the works of the Canal, obstruction thereto, or damage to other vessels which may be occasioned thereby.

XVII.—If any person or persons shall wantonly, or without cause and authority of the Sluice-keeper or Superintendent of the Canal, unmoor any vessel within the said Canal or Basins, or cut, or cast off, or break any rope, chain, or other fastening attached to the same, such person or persons shall for every such offence, forfeit and pay the sum of *five pounds*, and shall moreover be liable to make good all damage or loss which may ensue, in consequence of such act, either to the vessel or cargo, or to the said Canal and works.

XVIII.—No timber shall be floated on any part of the Canal or Basins, nor any cargo landed, discharged, or transhipped from or into any vessel, excepting at such places and at such times (other than the places mentioned in the Act), without special leave of the Wharfinger, or some authorized officer or servant of the Chamber of Exeter, under the penalty of *five pounds*.

XIX.—Whenever any trading-vessel or boat shall, by its quickness upon the Canal, come up with any other trading-vessel, boat, or barge, passing more slowly, every Master, Bargeman, Boatman, or person having the conduct of any such slower vessel, boat, or barge, shall stop and permit such other swifter trading vessel, boat, or barge to pass, so that no interruption may arise to such last mentioned vessels, boats, or barges, on pain of forfeiting for every such offence the sum of *one pound*.

XX.—If any person or persons shall put down without a handling, or carelessly with a handling, any or either of the head or tail cloughs belonging to any of the locks on the said Canal, such person or persons shall, for each and every offence, forefeit and pay the sum of *two pounds*.

XXI.—Any Master, Bargeman, Boatman, or other person having the command of any vessel, and allowing any such vessel, barge, lighter, or boat to pass in or upon the said Canal without having the sails of any such vessel *furled*, to forfeit and pay *five pounds* for each offence.

XXII.—Any person who shall throw stones, sand, gravel, ballast, or other rubbish or substance into any part of the Canal, Basins, or into any weir, trenches, or water-courses belonging thereto, shall forfeit and pay for every such offence the sum of *two pounds*.

XXIII.—If any Master, Owner, Bargeman, Boatman, or other person having the command, charge, or direction of any barge, lighter, or vessel, (other than a boat,) shall permit or suffer such vessel, barge, or lighter to enter or leave any lock without having fully opened both pair of any lock gates, such Master, Owner, Bargeman, Boatman, or other person shall, for each and every such offence, forfeit and pay the sum of *two pounds*.

XXIV.—If any driver, or other person having the care or guidance of any horse or other beast towing any vessel, barge, or boat on the said canal, shall neglect or refuse to take the water side of the towing-path with such horse or other beast when passed by or passing any person or persons on foot or riding, such driver or other person having the guidance or direction of the said horse or other beast shall, for each and every such offence, forfeit and pay the sum of *ten shillings*.

XXV.—No person shall heat any pitch, tar, turpentine, tallow, or other inflammable substance on board of any ship \or vessel within the Canal or Basins, or the entrances of the same; and any person or persons so offending shall forfeit and pay, for every such offence, the sum of *ten shillings*.

XXVI.—The utmost care is to be at all times taken of fires and lights on board vessels using the Canal or Basins, in order to guard against accident or mischief therefrom; and the officers and servants of the canal are strictly enjoined in case they shall witness on board of any vessels a negligent, careless, or improper conduct with regard to fires or lights, immediately to require the same to be extinguished, or report the circumstance to the Wharfinger, and in case the Master, Owner, or other person having charge of such vessel shall neglect or refuse so to extinguish such fires or lights, he or they shall, for every such offence forfeit and pay the sum of *ten shillings*.

XXVII.—No fire shall be made on the banks of the canal, or on the space adjoining the wharfs or basins, within thirty yards at the least of any vessel that may be therein, or in such a way as to cause danger or apprehension therefrom. Any person or persons offending against this bye-law shall, for every such offence, forfeit and pay the sum of *ten shillings*.

XXXVIII.—Any Collector, Sluice-keeper, Superintendent of the Canal, or other Officers of the Mayor and Chamber of the City of Exeter, taking or receiving any fee or reward of any kind whatsoever from any person or persons using the Canal, other than such as are prescribed by the Act of Parliament, to forfeit the sum of *five pounds* for every offence.

XXIX.—Any Master, Owner, or other person belonging to any ship or vessel entering or using the Canal and works, who shall have cause for complaint against any Wharfinger, Collector, Sluice-keeper, or other person belonging to or employed on the said Canal, is to leave the same in writing at the Wharfinger's Office, under cover to the *Receiver-General* or to the *Chamberlain* of the City of Exeter, in order that such redress may be afforded, and such steps taken thereon as may be expedient.

XXX.—No Boatman, Bargeman, Waterman, or other person shall use any shaft, staff, or other instrument, spiked or shod with iron or other metal, against any of the locks, bridges, or tunnels, or other brick or stone works, or any of the sides, or banks, or bottom of the said Canal, on pain of forfeiting, for every such offence, the sum of *five pounds*.

XXXI.—No person or persons navigating or being on board any vessel, boat, or barge upon the said Canal shall use, in or upon, or in any way attached to any such vessel, boat, or barge, any net or engine whatsoever for the taking, killing, or destroying any fish, under the penalty of *one pound* for every offence.

XXXII.—If any Master, Owner, Boatman, Bargeman, or other person shall fasten or cause to be fastened any tow-line or other rope belonging to any vessel, boat, or barge navigating on the said Canal, to any of the locks or other works belonging to the same, except to the regular and proper mooring posts, such Master, Owner, Boatman, Bargeman, or other person shall, for every such offence, forfeit and pay the sum of *five pounds*.

XXXIII.—If any person or persons whomsoever shall improperly or negligently leave open any gate or gates, or fasten down any drop-stiles on any of the towing-paths or other works belonging to and adjoining the said Canal, such person or persons shall, for each and every such offence, forfeit and pay the sum of *one pound*.

XXXIV.—If any person or persons whomsoever shall permit or suffer any horse or other beast, pig, cattle, or animal of any description, to trespass on or injure any of the towing or other paths, or any of the works belonging to the Canal or Basins, such person or persons shall, for each and every such offence, forfeit and pay the sum of *ten shillings*.

XXXV.—Every person whomsoever who shall drown, or throw, or cause to be drowned or thrown, any dog or cat, or any nuisance into any part of the Canal, Basins, or other works, shall for every such offence, forfeit and pay the sum of *five shillings*.

XXXVI.—All Masters, Owners, and Managers of Ships, &c., entering the Exeter Canal, are required under a penalty of *five pounds,* to deliver at the Wharfinger's Office, immediately upon their arrival at Exeter Quay or Basin, an account in writing of the several quantities, qualities, and weight of the goods, wares, merchandize, and things contained in every such ship, &c., and to whom the same are consigned, which said penalty will in future be enforced in all cases of omission so to do.

XXXVII.—In case of neglect or refusal to pay the rates, tolls, or duties, the Wharfinger is empowered to detain any ship, vessel, or craft, and the boats and tackle thereof; or distrain the goods, wares, merchandize, or commodities, for or in respect of which such tolls, rates, or duties, respectively, ought to have been paid.

By Order and under the Common Seal of the Mayor, Bailiffs, and Commonalty of the City of Exeter, at a Chamber, held at the Guildhall, Exeter, 17th August, 1829.

EDWD. GATTEY, Town-Clerk.

A BRIEF BIBLIOGRAPHY

A comprehensive list of sources is given in the 'Notes' section of this book. The following, all published in recent years, are recommended for further study:

The City

Hoskins, William G., *Industry, Trade and People in Exeter, 1688–1800*, 1968.
Hoskins, William G., *Two Thousand Years in Exeter*, 1970.
Newton, Robert, *Victorian Exeter*, 1968.
Stephens, William B., *Seventeenth Century Exeter*, 1958.

The Exeter Canal

Clark, Edwin, A. G., *The Ports of the Exe Estuary, 1660–1860*, 1968.
Hadfield, Charles, *The Canals of South West England*, 1967.

The Railways

Maggs, C. G., *Railways to Exmouth*, 1980.
Marshall, C. F. Dendy, *A History of the Southern Railway*, 1964.
McDermot, Edward T., *History of the Great Western Railway*, 1964.
Thomas, David St John, *A Regional History of the Railways of Great Britain: Vol. I—The West Country*, 4th edn., 1973.

Industrial Archaeology

Chitty, Michael, *Industrial Archaeology of Exeter*, 1974.

The Port of Topsham

Bradbeer, D. M., *The Story of the Manor and Port of Topsham*, 1968.
Ponsford, Clive N., *Topsham and the Exe Estuary*, 1979.

INDEX

LIST OF SUBSCRIBERS

Major A. A. Anderson
Dr. J. R. Andrews
George Astbury
Penny Ballinger
David Banks
A. B. Barber
Jancis Bateman
Bruce A. Bearne
C. W. Beckerleg
Maurice I. Berrill
Brian W. F. Berrington
Graeme Black
Blundell's School Library
David H. Boakes, C Eng, MI Mech E
J. M. Bolton
John Bosanko
T. & J. C. Boughton
Michael Rome Bouquet
R. Chester Browne
K. J. Burrow
Fraser Clift
D. L. Cockin
College of St Mark & St John,
     Plymouth
Brian G. Coward
Arnold J. Cox
William E. Cox
James L. Cunnington
Philip Daniell
Devon & Exeter Institution
Susan Dorothy Dunlop
J. E. Dunn
Mrs. J. Edmonds
David Edmund
Mr. & Mrs. D. Eggleston
Roger Evans
Thomas Alexander Meade Falkner
H. S. A. Fox

David W. Gale
Eric Garland
Mrs. M. A. Gentry
Captain B. M. Glover
J. Lloyd Griffith
Michael Handford
Robert Harris
Denis C. Harward, TD
Graham Hawkins, MA
Brian R. Heal
D. Heaton
John & Jeanne Hodgkinson
Gilbert Holder
Bernard Moynihan Holland
Denys Hutchings
Rosemary Huxtable
Keith Martyn James
J. L. Jervoise
Miss Anne Farewell Jones
Christopher J. Kelly
T. J. Lambert
Rosemary Leach
John P. Leyland
Dr. E. D. Lindsay
G. W. Lloyd
Richard N. Longridge
J. H. Luxton
Arnold W. H. Madge
Magdalen College Library, Oxford
Mr. & Mrs. B. Martin
J. A. Meer
Nicholas Melchior
Paul Methven
David Neil Morris, B Sc
David Morrish
Ian & Pat Moss
The North Devon Athenaeum

Mr. R. O. Nott
A. Parker
Margaret Parkinson
Ian R. Patterson
H. T. E. Pepperall
Eric Picketts
John C. de V. Roberts
J. A. C. Robins
Neil C. Rumbol
F. A. & S. M. Rymell
Peter Sainsbury
Robert George Seabrook
T. W. Sedgwick
Dr. R. R. Sellman
Dr. R. A. Shove
Rosalind D. Smallwood
Gregory & Pamela Smith
Mrs. Mary Smyth
Dr. Roger W. Squires
Jeffrey Stanyer
Marian Stephens
J. A. Stratton
D. L. B. Thomas
Graham Thorne
Dickson & Miriam Tolman
A. R. Tulley
Norah & Ron Turner
Frederick W. Venn
T. W. Vernon-Smith
Alan P. Voce
Frederick John Vosper
P. D. Webley
Mrs. E. J. Welch
Peter L. White
Mrs. Vere Wight-Boycott
Teresa Williams
Ian J. Wilson